EXCEL 2020

Learn Excel Essential Skills with Smart Method—Learn the Basics of Excel in 30 Minutes—When You Improve with Excel 2020, You Feel like a Computer Artist

Alex Parker

DISCLAIMER

The author and any editors of this book do not guarantee the accuracy and completeness of the information in this work and cannot be held responsible for any errors in the text.

The sources of the contents are always indicated, when present. The author assumes no responsibility for any reported inaccuracies.

Although every effort has been made to ensure that the information in this publication is correct, the reader must understand that this book's contents are the result of the study, professional experience, and research by the author.

Therefore, sometimes, the contents of the book can be the reflection of his personal opinions.

Regarding this text, readers are invited to respond according to their judgment on the individual personal circumstances and act accordingly.

It is important to highlight that there are no guarantees of achieving a secure income or guiding results following what the author has written in the books of practical advice.

The reader must always inquire through legally recognized specialized professionals and always comply with the law.

Table of Contents

INTRODUCTION

Microsoft Excel is a popular Microsoft spreadsheet program. It is planned for machines utilizing the Windows operating system as well as for devices using Mac OS. It has a user-friendly GUI and a variety of resources that can rapidly and efficiently construct a map.

Through tandem with a strong publicity strategy, Excel has become one of the world's most successful software programs. Excel is normally packaged into the software kit of Microsoft Office.

Excel is not Microsoft's first spreadsheet program. In 1982, the firm first launched a table named Multiplan, which gradually lost market share due to Lotus 1-2-3. As a result, Microsoft wanted to build a program that could contend successfully against Lotus's domination.

The very first Excel edition was introduced in 1985 and was released on the Pc. Two years later, the first version for Windows would be released. Because Lotus could not bring their tablet program to Windows fast enough, Excel starts to gain a bigger market share.

Excel had exceeded 1-2-3 by 1988, and it is one of the factors behind Microsoft's success as a software company. An Excel file in the form of.xls must arrive. There are some changes to the program GUI, but it should still consist of rows and columns. Data may be stored in cells that influence the details that might occur in certain cells.

In comparison, Excel allows the user a lot of power over the look and details of the cells. Microsoft Word and PowerPoint have all been developed to conform to Excel.

The implementation of Visual Basic with Excel has provided for the automation of a variety of tasks. Since 1993, Visual Basic and the implementation of an interactive software framework shape an important part of Excel.

However, Excel's programmed properties of Visual Basic resulted in some macro viruses, but traditional antivirus programs now disable all of them. Microsoft also enables users to deactivate macros' use if they choose, eliminating the problem in large measure.

Although Microsoft Excel was not well known in the late 1980s, it has become the most widely distributed software, although some companies, especially Google, face competition. Nevertheless, with the introduction of Excel, Microsoft rendered its mark and next to Windows, one of the most popular software products globally.

It has outstanding estimation methods, which can also be used effectively for graphics. Nonetheless, if Multiplan had not been the mentor that began it all, the company wouldn't have the influence it now has.

UNDERSTANDING MICROSOFT EXCEL

What Is Excel?

Microsoft Excel is a spreadsheet program that enables users to place, modify, and manage data in a database-like category called a workbook. A workbook utilizes a series of worksheets to arrange data into a structure or row and separate columns into rows. Users should insert details or numbers in such cells such that basic or complicated calculations should accurately be measured. In their workbook, users will insert artifacts like diagrams and graphs to depict their entered data in several special ways graphically.

Who Created Excel?

The Microsoft Corporation developed Microsoft Excel in 1984. It has been designed to create a more efficient way for users to calculate data without dealing with the DOS command line. It was initially developed to be used on Apple computers. Microsoft Excel was one of the first programs created for Microsoft Windows when

Microsoft Windows was first launched in 1987. It was the first windows-based table program until 1992.

Versions

For three different operating systems, Microsoft Excel has created several different versions. From 1987 up to now, Microsoft Windows had 11 different versions from 1985 until now.

Features

Microsoft Excel has built a range of apps to support Excel users since the software was originally established. Features such as algorithms, tables, charts, maps, sorting, and filtering have rendered it a resource with several specific uses that reach, manage, and view data within Excel. New functionality such as pivot tables, import and export choices, and visual framework for applications has encouraged and rendered customizing the whole method of using Excel.

Tools

Microsoft Excel has also built helpful menus and software to help further Excel users customize their Excel applications and workbooks. The fast access toolbar has been created to enable users to access commonly used commands quickly.

You may configure this toolbar by Excel framework or a similar workbook. Excel also developed the ribbon to replace the existing Excel menu models. The belt enabled Excel users to customize the belt to meet their specific requirements.

File Types

Microsoft Excel has created new ways of saving workbooks and different Excel files. Through generating a new form of protecting Excel data, the import and export function enables Excel users to quickly import workbooks, data, export workbooks, or files that have already been developed, which could be used later on.

WHY LEARN MICROSOFT EXCEL?

We are all dealing in one way or the other with numbers. We also have regular expenses that we compensate for from our monthly profits. To invest wisely, you have to learn your revenue and expenditures. Microsoft Excel is useful for capturing, reviewing, and storing these statistical details.

Where Can I Get Microsoft Excel?

There are many options to get Microsoft Excel. You may buy it from a computer hardware store which also sells applications. Software Excel is part of the system suite Microsoft Office. Alternatively, you can download the license key from the Microsoft website.

How to Open Microsoft Excel?

Excel programming isn't unlike operating any other Windows software. If you run Windows with such a GUI (Windows XP, Vista, and 7), follow the steps below.

- Click on the start menu

- Point to all programs

- Point to Microsoft Excel

- Click on Microsoft Excel

Alternatively, if placed there, you can even access it from the start tab. If you have built one, you may also access it from the mobile shortcut. We will operate with Windows 8.1 and Microsoft Excel 2019 (currently the latest in 2020) for this part. Follow the measures below to run Excel under Windows 8 or 10.

- Click on the start menu

- Search for Excel N.B. even before you even typing; all programs starting with what you have typed will be listed.

- Click on Microsoft Excel

Understanding the Ribbon

The ribbon gives shortcuts for Excel commands. An order is an operation executed by the device; a command example is to create a new document, print documentation, etc. The following picture displays the ribbon used in Excel 2019.

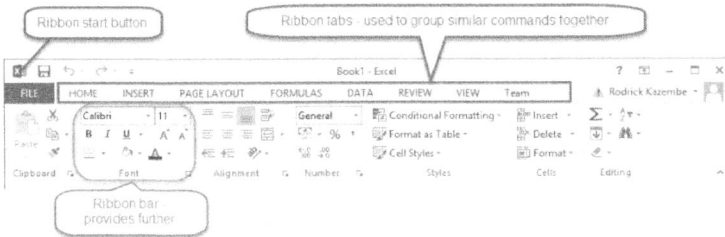

Ribbon Components Explained

- **Ribbon start button** – The commands are used, i.e., to generate fresh papers, save current jobs, print, use the Excel-customization tools, etc.

- **Ribbon tabs** – The tabs are used together to combine related commands. The home tab is used to format data for basic commands, for example, to make it more presentable, sort, and find specific data in the spreadsheet.

- Ribbon bar – The bars are used together to similar group commands. For example, the ribbon bar of Alignment is used to organize all commands used to coordinate data.

Understanding the Worksheet (Rows and Columns, Sheets, Workbooks)

A worksheet is a series of columns and rows. They shape a cell when a row and a column cross. Data storage cells are used. Every cell is marked with a cell address. Usually, columns are marked with letters, and rows are generally numbered.

A workbook is a worksheet set. It has three Excel cells by chance. You may delete or install additional sheets to match your needs. The sheets are numbered by design Sheet1, Sheet2, and so on. It would help if you converted the sheet's name into real words, i.e., regular expenses, weekly schedule, etc.

Customization Microsoft Excel Environment

I like the black color myself, and my excellent theme appears blackish. Your favorite color could be blue, so you, too, can make your theme look blue. You do not want to use ribbon buttons, e.g., the author, because you are not a programmer. Everything is possible through customizations. We must glance at this sub-section.

Customization the Ribbon

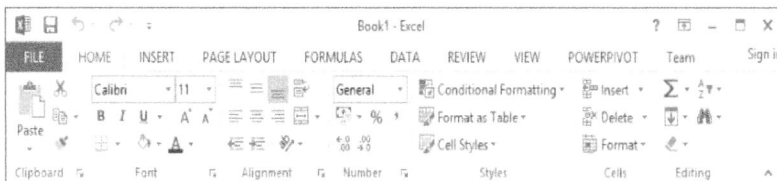

- Setting the color theme

- Settings for formulas

- Proofing settings

- Save settings

The image above shows the default Excel 2019 ribbon. Let's continue with ribbon modification, presume you don't want to display any of the ribbon tabs or attach a few missing tabs such as the developer tab. To do this, you can use the options window.

Click on the Ribbon Start Button

Choose from the drop-down menu options. You should be able to see a dialog for Excel Options.

Choose the ribbon option from the left side panel sees below.

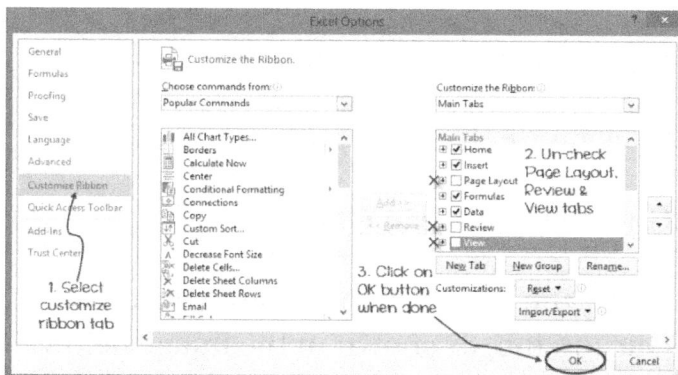

- Delete checkpoints from the tabs you do not like to use on the label on your hand. We have deleted the Page Layout, Review, and View tab for this example.

- Click on the "OK" button when you are done.

- Your ribbon will look as follows.

Adding Custom Tabs to the Ribbon

You can also add your tab, give it a personalized name and, assign commands. Let's add a line to the Guru99 document ribbon.

- Right-click and pick Ribbon Design. The above dialog window will appear.

- Click on the new tab button, as illustrated in the animated image below.

- Select the newly created tab.

- Click on the Rename button.

- Give it the name of Guru99.

- Select the New Group (Custom) under the Guru99 tab, as shown in the image below.

- Click on the Rename button and give it the name of My Commands.

- Let's now add commands to my ribbon bar.

- The commands are listed on the middle panel.

- Select the All chart types command and clicks on the Add button.

- Click on OK.

Setting the Color Theme

You need to go to the Excel ribbon to configure the color-theme for your Excel sheet and click on the File à Option button. It must open a browser to obey the steps below.

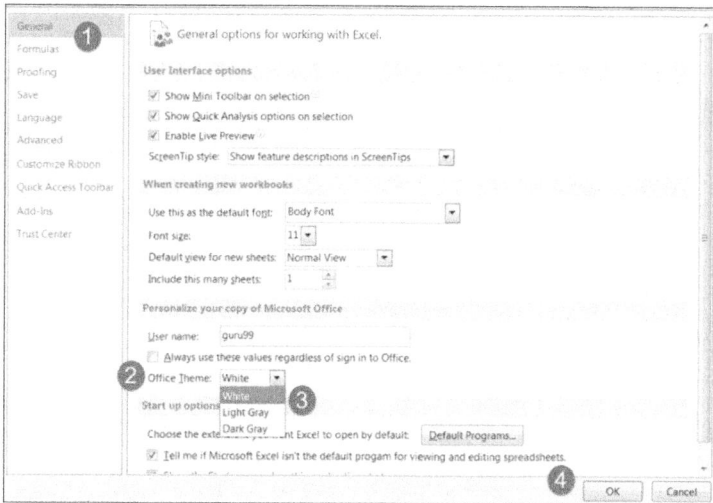

- The general tab on the left-hand panel will be selected by default.

- Look for a color scheme under General options for working with Excel.

31

- Click on the color scheme drop-down list and select the desired color.

- Click on the OK button.

Settings for Formulas

This choice helps you to describe how Excel functions for formulas. You will use it to set preferences, i.e., automatically full layout, adjust the cell comparison type to use the column to row numbers, and other features.

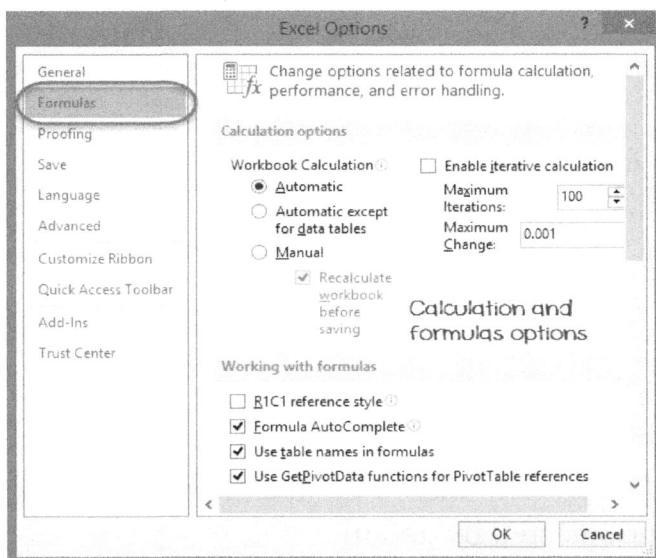

Click on the checkbox if you want to trigger a function. If you wish to disable an alternative, delete the checkbox symbol. This choice is accessible from the Options dialog in the Method tab from the left-hand column.

Proofing Settings

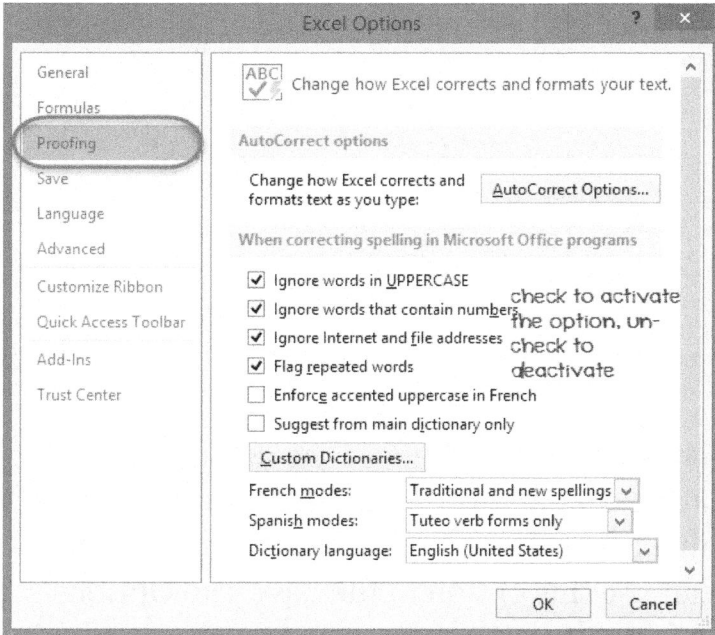

It alternative manipulates the input text in Excel. It enables setting choices like dictionary vocabulary to be used while searching for incorrect spellings, dictionary tips, etc. This choice can be accessed from the dialog window under the check tab in the left-hand panel.

Save Settings

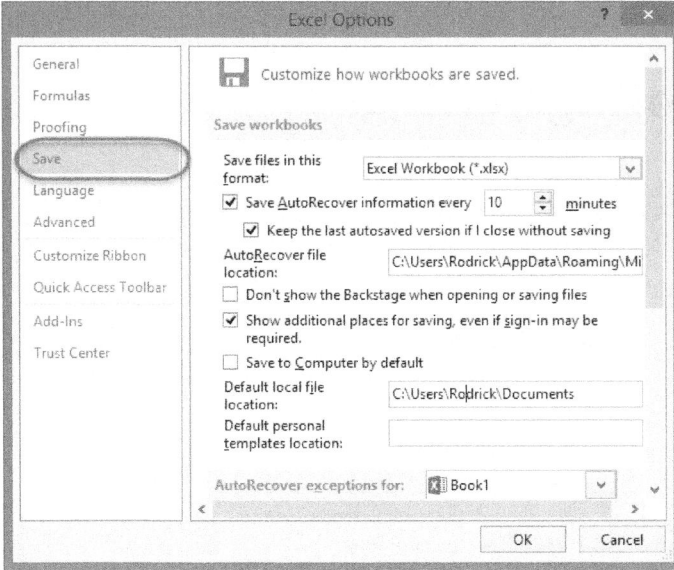

This choice helps you choose the default file format for file saving, make auto-recovery if your machine falls off before you can save your job, etc. You can use this option in the Save Tab Options dialog from the left panel.

Important Excel Shortcuts

- Ctrl + P: used to open the print dialogue window.

- Ctrl + N: creates a new workbook.

- Ctrl + S: saves the current workbook.

- Ctrl + C: copy contents of current select.

- Ctrl + V: paste data from the clipboard.

- SHIFT + F3: displays the function insert dialog window.

- SHIFT + F11: Creates a new worksheet.

- F2: Check formula and cell range covered.

Best Practices when Working with Microsoft Excel

1. Save a backward-compatible workbook. When you do not need the new functionality of higher Excel models, save the files for backward compatibility of 2003*.xls format.

2. Use column and worksheet overview titles in a workbook.

3. Consider dealing with several variables in complicated calculations. Attempt to split them into limited controlled outcomes from which you can create.

4. Whenever you can use built-in functions instead of writing your formulas.

Microsoft Excel is a powerful spreadsheet program used to record, manipulate, store, and customize numerical data according to your preferences. The ribbon is used for running specific Excel functions. With the menu options, you can customize several items, e.g., ribbon, formula, test, save, etc.

HOW TO ENTER BASIC FORMULAS AND CALCULATIONS IN EXCEL?

If you are starting with Excel, it is one of the first things you should learn to create formulas. This tutorial shows you how to construct basic Excel formulas and calculations.

Excel is a massive calculator at its core. Indeed, it is an easy way of thinking about Excel to treat every cell as a single calculator in a worksheet. An Excel table contains millions of cells, which means that you can work with millions of individual computers.

You will also just construct formulas that bind various cells together (e.g., apply value to the cell number). You may construct formulas that bind cells together in various worksheets. And you can also build procedures that bind cells together in multiple workbooks.

How to Enter a Formula in Excel?

Every cell in Excel will contain a measurement. They term this a method in Excel jargon. Will cell can have one formula. By inserting formula in a box, Excel will measure the outcome and give you the equation's outcome.

Yes, Excel can recalculate the product of all cells in the worksheet after entering a formula in every cell. It is typically achieved in the blink of an eye so that you don't generally feel it, but you might note that it can take longer to recalculate huge and complicated tablets.

You will make sure the Excel understands what you intend to do before entering a calculation. You begin by typing the sign = (equal), then the rest of your formula.

Instead, Excel suggests that you enter either a number or a letter when you don't first enter a symbol of equal importance.

You may start a formula either with a plus (+) symbol or a minus (-). Excel suggests that you select a formula and apply the same symbol.

1	You type	The result
2	10+10	20
3	100-50	50
4	10*10	100
5	100/5	20

There are four simple formulas in this example:

- Addition (+)

- Subtraction (-)

- Multiplication (*)

- Division (/)

In each scenario, type the equal sign (=), then click Enter to tell Excel that you've done.

- Excel will sometimes display a warning instead of simply entering your form. That occurs if the calculation becomes incorrect, i.e., it is not accepted in a format by Excel. This would typically always inform you of what you did wrong.

- Other times, Excel may enter the correct formula and then show you an error such as # VALUE. This means that you entered a valuable formula, but Excel couldn't determine a valid result from your formula.

Creating Formulas that Refer to other Cells in the same Worksheet

The power of Excel is that you can create formulas that refer to values in other cells.

You can see the top (A, B) and bottom (1,2,3,4,5) headings in the illustration above. In integrating this meaning, each cell in a worksheet has a specific connection (A1, A2, A3, B1, B2, B3, and so forth).

When creating a formula, you could use these cell references to refer to other cells to add values into a formula in other cells. The value in a different cell could be a simple number or a cell containing a formula.

If you build a formula that applies to another cell that already has a formula, that formula's product is included in the other cell.

If you change the result of the formula in that other cell, your formula will also change. Here are some examples of certain Excel formulas referring to other cells:

	A	B
1	you type	the result
2	10+10	20
3	100-50	50
4	10*10	100
5	100/5	20
6	B2+B3	70
7	B4-B5	80
8	B5*B2	400
9	B8/B3	8

Rows 6-8 draw on previous examples in this example to bind cells together:

- B6 combines B2 and B3 values. If you change one of the values in B2 or B3, you will also change the result in B6.

- B7 and B8 subtract and multiply the values in other cells.

- B9 continues a step and divides B8 into B3. Note that B8 multiplied B5 and B2 in turn. This means that increasing the values of either B5 or B2 creates a domino effect where the value of B8 increases, and thus the value of B9 always shifts. Note that when you finish entering a change in either B5 or B2, Excel handles it all.

Creating Formulas that Refer to Cells in other Worksheets

You begin with a single worksheet when you first open Excel. Excel allows you to have more than one worksheet in a single table file (known as a workbook). In fact, in previous versions of Excel, a new workbook with three worksheets automatically began.

Earlier, we saw how to connect two cells in a worksheet using their cell reference value. It functions just the same to connect to a cell in another worksheet, but we need to include further detail on the cell's position so that Excel understands this is the cell.

Here are some examples of formulas in the same workbook that refer to cells in another worksheet:

you type	the result
B8/B3	8
B9*Data!A2	32
Data!A4/B9	4.25

The formulas in B10 and B11 refer in this example to cells in another worksheet called Data.

- B10 multiplies the value by cell A2 in B9 in the data worksheet.

- B11 takes the A4 value from the Data worksheet and splits it into B9.

In other words, we told Excel to go to our Data worksheet and use the values in our formulas in that worksheet.

There are a few ways to create such formulas:

- Type the formula manually. In the above instance, by taping the name of a worksheet followed by an exclamation (!) The other worksheet's reference would be created; the exclamation mark says that Excel is referring to another worksheet.

- Start to type the formula by typing the same sign (=), then click on the other worksheet name. Excel switches to the other worksheet, and you can click on the cell in your form. You can then press Enter to complete the form, or you can click on the original name of the sheet and finish the form before pressing Enter.

Note that if you change the Data worksheet, the Data formats must immediately upgrade to match the new name. Here are the above examples if the name of the worksheet Data is changed to Daily Data.

you type	the result
B8/B3	8
B9*Data!A2	32
Data!A4/B9	4.25

Note how Excel has put the apostrophes around the name of the Daily Data worksheet. It is attributable to the room in the context of the worksheet. Excel must make sure that the equation fits still; if you write the formula manually without the apostrophes, Excel cannot verify the calculation and does not allow you to access it.

Creating Formulas that Link to Other Workbooks

As you can imagine what we've already covered, you may also construct a cell format in another workbook (i.e., another file). Again, it is just a question of referring the cell in the other workbook correctly.

The example below shows how this looks:

	you type	the result
3	B8/B3	8
.0	B9*Daily Data!A2	32
.1	Daily Data!A4/B9	4.25
.2	B9*[Excel-data-table-xlsx]Data!SDSG	48

In this case, B12 includes a formula that refers to D6 in a worksheet named Data in an Excel-data-table-xlsx format.

The brackets of the square are used for the filename, i.e., [filename]. Be aware that if the mentioned file is not currently open. The brackets can also contain a complete file path to this file to allow Excel to read still the cell value referred to even if the file isn't open.

The Apostrophes Are Used to Enclose the Full File Name and Worksheet Name

Excel then uses absolute references to identify the cell to which it refers. This means that your formula still works if you move (not copy) the contents of the cell D6 in the datasheet. The $signs (instead of a relative reference) are used to denote an absolute reference. Absolute and relative references are not within this lesson, but you can read about them in this lesson.

Excel formulas learning is one of the most important things that you will learn to do with Excel. Hopefully, this lesson has put you on the right track, and in no time will you create tables with formulas of your own.

HOW TO SELECT, ACTIVATE AND EDIT CELLS IN EXCEL?

The most basic actions anybody can do in a worksheet are to select, activate, and edit cells. As an Excel user, you must be able to start and maintain a cell when entering data. Also, you must first trigger the activated cell code. But not everybody knows what an active cell is. So, we're going to begin there:

What Is an Active Cell?

An active cell is just a rectangular box that shows the cell in a tablet. It helps us to identify the cell where data is entered that we are currently working on. An active cell is often called a cell tracker, a current cell, or a cell picked.

100	activecell address	40	0
100	activate cell excel	200	0
100	activecell address vba	30	1
100	active cell in excel	200	1
100	active cell definition excel	150	1

Fig 1: Activating a cell in excel

Each Excel user needs to understand the difference between the cell activated and the edit mode. For this reason, you must learn how to activate a cell.

Activating a Cell

When you click on a cell, it just means you activate it. Around it, you will see a thick green/gray border. An active cell indicates it's ready for editing because we see how a cell can be set to edit mode.

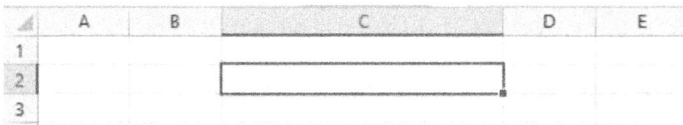

Fig 2: Selecting a cell

In figure 2 above, you have just clicked on the C2 cell. You may either shift the cursor and press on another cell or use the down, up, left, and right arrow keys for the current cell shift. Also, the active cell row should move downward when you click the Enter key. If you want to make some changes to the cell, you will need to manually select it again before you put it in edit mode.

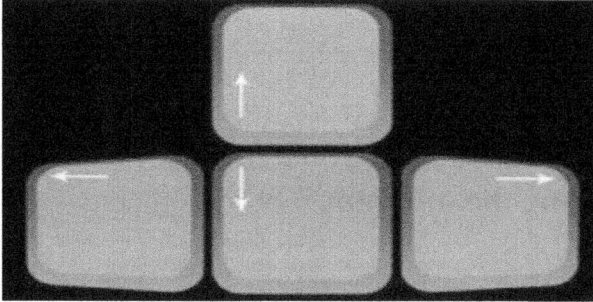

Fig 3: Arrow Keys

Additional methods are often essential for triggering a cell, such as typing the cell connection in the top "Name Box."

How to Insert an Excel Cell in 'Edit Mode?'

As mentioned, activating a cell doesn't mean it is ready to edit. There are three methods through which a cell can be edited.

The first approach is to double-click the cell you want to edit. This is the most common and possibly the most common method. Double-clicking on a cell will just trigger and edit it.

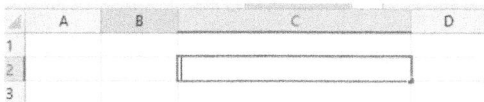

Fig 4: Cursor in an active cell

You can also edit a cell by clicking on the formula bar. This method only works if the cell that you want to edit is active. Before heading for the formula bar, make sure you highlight and select the cell using the different methods discussed above.

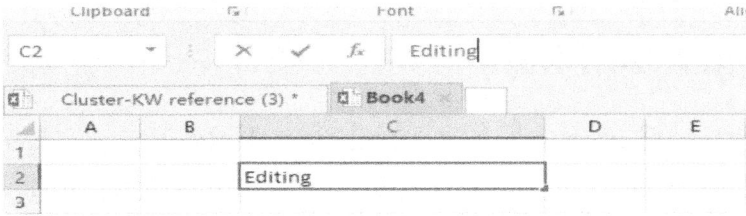

Fig 5: Editing a cell

The other way to edit a cell is by simply pressing F2.

How to Keep the Active Cell in Excel?

After entering data in Excel and pressing "Enter," the activated cell moves directly under it to the cell. This is usually fine, but it can be annoying, for example, if you work on a formula and check the results. It is also easy to get lost in a large tablet.

For instance, if you use Excel to monitor the orders, this table may become very large, and you can easily lose your position if you scroll off the active cell to find out something else. Excel has solutions to these two problems, however.

Keeping the Cell after Completing an Operation

Step 1

Start Excel and load the table you are working on.

Step 2

Click on the 'File' tab in the upper left corner of the screen, and then click 'Options.' From the left menu of the window that appears, click on 'Advanced' and then uncheck the 'Move Selection after Enter Pressing.' When you're done, click "OK."

Step 3

Go back to your worksheet and type your data and tap Enter. This finishes the process and recovers each term's value, but retains the current cell chosen instead of switching to the one below.

Returning to the Active Cell

Step 1

startup Excel and open your spreadsheet.

Step 2

Click on any cell.

Step 3

Remove the active cell, so it's off-screen.

Step 4

Press simultaneously "Ctrl" and "Backspace." This returns the screen to the active node. Whenever you move away from the active cell and forget where it is, you can use this. Notice that any worksheet has an active cell of its own.

USING FIND AND REPLACE IN EXCEL

Use the Find and Replace functions in Excel to look for something, such as a number or text string, in your workbook. You can either find or replace the search item with something else. You can include wildcards in your search terms, such as questions, tildes, and asterisks or numbers.

You can search through rows and columns, search through comments and values, and search through worksheets or entire workbooks.

Find

Looking for something, press Ctrl+F, or go to Home >Editing > Find & Select > Find.

- **Note:** The following illustration demonstrates the whole Find dialog by clicking on the Options >> icon. It will display hidden options by default.

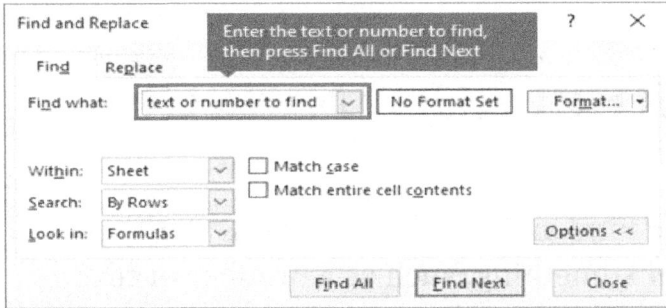

Find and Replace dialog box with the following elements:
- Tabs: Find, Replace
- Find what: text or number to find | No Format Set | Format...
- Within: Sheet
- Search: By Rows
- Look in: Formulas
- Match case
- Match entire cell contents
- Options <<
- Buttons: Find All | Find Next | Close
- Tooltip: Enter the text or number to find, then press Find All or Find Next

1. In the Find what: Box, type text or numbers to locate, or in the Locate what: tab, click on the arrow and then choose from the list a recent scan.

Tips: You can use wildcard characters — the question mark (?), an asterisk (*), tilde (~) — in your search criteria.

- Use the question mark (?) to find a single character — e.g., s? t finds 'sat' and 'set.'

- Use the asterisk (*) to find many characters — such as "sad" and "started" find by s*d.

- Use the equivalent tilde (~)? *, or ~ to find question marks, asterisks, or other tilde signs, e.g., fy91~? Searches for "fy91?".

2. Click Find All or Find Next to run your search.

Tip: once you clicked on Find All, each occurrence of the criteria you are looking for will

54

be listed, and the cell selected by clicking on a certain occurrence in the list. You will filter the search results by clicking on a column title.

3. Click Options>> to refine your search further if needed:

- **Within:** Select Sheet or Workbook to search for data in a worksheet or a full workbook.

- **Search:** You can decide to search by Rows (default) or by Columns.

- **Look in:** For specific information, click on Formulas, Values, Notes, or Comments in this box.

Note: Formulas, Values, Notes, and Comments are available only on the Find tab; only Formulas can be found on the Replace tab.

- **Match case** – you need this to check for case-sensitive data.

- **Match entire cell contents** - Check this if you are looking for cells that contain only the characters you typed in the Find what: box.

4. For specific formatting text or numbers: click Format and then make your selections in the Find Format dialog box.

Tip: You can delete all criteria in the Finding what box if you want to find cells matching just one format and then select a certain cell format as an example. Click the format file next to the format, click on Cell Format and click on the cell with the formatting you want to find.

Replace

To replace a text or a numbers, press Ctrl+H, or go to Home > Editing > Find & Select > Replace.

Note: The following illustration demonstrates the whole Find dialog by clicking on the Options >> icon. It will display hidden options by default.

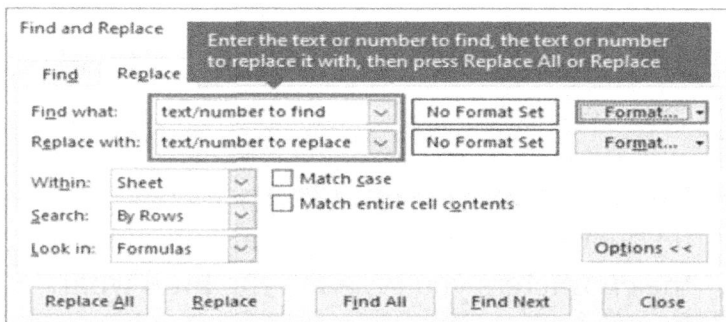

In the Find what: box, type in the text or numbers that you want to find, or click on the arrow Find what: box, and select a new search item.

Tips: You can use wildcard characters — the question mark (?), an asterisk (*), tilde (~) — in your find requirement.

- Make use of the question mark (?) to locate any single character —for example, s?t finds "sat" and "set."

- Make use of the asterisk (*) to locate any number of characters —for example, s*d finds "sad" and "started."

- Make use of the tilde (~) followed by? *, or ~ to locate question marks, asterisks, or other tilde characters —for example, fy91~? Finds "fy91?".

In the Replace with: box, Enter the preferred text or numbers to substitute the search code.

1. Click Replace All or Replace

Tip: Clicking Replace All replaces every occurrence of the criteria you are looking for, while Replace updates one occurrence at a time.

2. Click Options>> to refine your search further if needed:

- Within: Select Sheet or Workbook to search for data in a worksheet or a full workbook.

- Search: use search by rows (default) or by columns.

- Look in: Click formula, Meanings, Remarks, or Comments to check for data with precise information.

Note: Formulas, Values, Notes, and Comments can only be found on the locate Find tab; only Formulas are available on the Replace tab.

- Match case - Check this if you want to search for case-sensitive data.

- Match entire cell contents - Check this if you want to search for cells containing just the characters you typed in the Find what: box.

If you wish to search for specific text or numbers, click Format and select it from the Find Format dialog.

Tip: You can delete all criteria in the Finding what box if you want to find cells matching just one format and then select a certain cell format as an example. Click the format file next to the format, click on Cell Format and click on the cell with the formatting you want to find.

CREATE AND MANAGE WORKBOOKS AND WORKSHEETS

The Microsoft (MS) Excel workbook is a file that can be stored and entered within the MS Excel application. There are multiple worksheets in a workbook. Each worksheet comprises several cells containing information about a specific subject and can be modified according to the requirements.

A workbook defines the data included in the worksheet. However, only worksheets on workbooks do manipulation of data. Every workbook has a separate window in Excel 2019. Working on workbooks or two monitors is easier as the workbook's name is shown in the title bar.

Typically, when we start a new project, we will build a new workbook. In Excel 2019, there are many ways to build a workbook:

- Create a workbook with a blank document

- Create a workbook from a template

- Open an existing workbook

Creating a Blank Excel Workbook

Users can create a new workbook with a blank document in Excel 2019. A new workbook based on the current workbook is also available. A new workbook includes three worksheets by design. However, we can also switch the number of worksheets as required in a workbook.

Create a Workbook from an Excel Template

A template is a pre-designed worksheet that can be modified to meet the needs of users. The Excel template includes predefined formulas and personalized formatting. It saves time and money in the work on a new project.

To create a workbook from a template, we must choose a suitable template as required. In addition to Microsoft, many individual users and third-party providers can create custom templates.

Open an Existing Excel Workbook

An existing workbook has already been saved and saved on the computer or the web. Existing workbooks can be opened from local computer disks, SkyDrive, online storage, and other online storage sites. SkyDrive is a Microsoft product, and everyone can sign in or register on SkyDrive online to store files.

Business Example

Alex was tasked with creating an inventory datasheet for the assets of his company. To do this, Microsoft Excel 2019 must work extensively. You must enter and edit data in your workbooks and start by creating a workbook.

See the description of the measures to launch an Excel workbook.

- Open Microsoft Excel and press the File tab to create a new worksheet.

- Click New and then press the choice Blank Workbook.

- To create a template workbook, under New, click the Search bar for Online templates and enter the template form required.

- Click on the icon Check.

- Choose one of the templates available and press Build.

- Click File to open an existing workbook, then press Close.

- Click Machine, then press Navigate.

- Go to the Excel file you want to open in the open pop-up window, select it, and click Open.

Native and Non-Native Files

Let's first understand what files are Native and Non-Native.

- The file format type that can be created or accepted by each software program is called native files.

- Non-native files are considered a software system that helps one function and transfer data in a specific format.

Most common native file format in Excel 2019:

- Excel Workbook(XLSX): It is the default Excel 2007-2019 XML-based file format.

- Excel Workbook (XLS): The default Excel 1997-2003 file format.

- Excel Standard Workbook(XLSB): The Excel 2007 to 2019 standard file format

- Excel Workbook Code(XLSM): The format for Excel 2007 to 2019 is XML-based and macro-enabled files.

- Excel Workbook Code(XLM): The macro-file format is used for earlier Excel versions. There are XLTS, XML (XML) and Excel Add-in (XLAM) files.

The top common non-native file format used in Excel are:

- text(.txt): It allows users to save a workbook as a text file with a tab. The user can save this file as compatible with Macintosh and the MS-DOS.

- Comma Separated Values (CSV): it gives the ability to save a text file as a comma. The consumer should keep it when the operating system is Macintosh and MS-DOS compliant.

Connecting or Importing External Files

In Excel 2019, periodic analysis of this data without repeated copying is the main advantage of connecting it to external data. Repeated copying is a time-consuming process that is vulnerable to error.

Connections to external data can be disabled on the computer by default. If this feature is to be used, then the external data connections from trust center settings must first be enabled.

Data are imported in two ways:

- **Delimited:** this choice is used in situations where the text contains the comma, line, semicolon, and other symbols.

- **Fixed Width:** now, this option is used when the length of all rows is similar.

We may link or import data from the following sources in Excel:

- **From Access:** This option allows easy access to MS Access databases, which store large amounts of information. After connecting to the access, the database has been entered in MS Excel; any changes in the access database will automatically update the Excel file.

- **From the Web:** This option enables access to website data such as share markets and lives currency converters. Copying data from the website to MS Excel is a time-consuming task. Excel makes it simple to import external website info.

- **From Text Files:** This choice provides access to files that are available in several operating systems in text format. Some of Excel's most popular data sources for connecting or importing analysis data, SQL server included analytics services, zero-marketplace windows, and Microsoft query.

External data can be imported in various ways:

- **Table:** It is a general table format for importing the data in rows and columns.

- **Pivot Table Report:** A pivot table report is a table format summary of the raw data. If this option is selected, the data is imported in the pivot table form.

- **Pivot Chart:** A pivot chart is used as a standard chart to represent data series, categories, and chart access. It also helps us to filter controls directly on the graph so that a data subset can be easily analyzed.

- The new feature introduced in Excel 2019 is the Power View Report. Power View is an interactive data scan, viewing, and presentation experience that promotes intuitive, ad hoc reporting.

- Only Create Connection: Establishes a link between the data source and the Excel file.

Business Example

Alex was assigned the task of inventing the data assets of his company. You will also need to use data from non-Excel files. He requires text files in Excel 2019 to be imported. He would also like to explore the External Data option in Excel.

Let's describe the file import phase in Excel:

- Click the Open item on the file tab to open a non-native file in Excel.

- Click on the computer and navigate.

- Navigate to the requested folder in the open pop-up window and select all files in the Combobox files.

- Select and click the required.txt or.csv file.

- Select the appropriate options from the text import wizard, click next and click finish.

- Click on the data tab to import external files.

- Choose the text option.

- Select the required text file in the import text of the pop-up window and click Import.

- Complete and finish the text import wizard steps.

- Select the destination of the imported text in the import dialog box and click OK.

- To import any changes made to a text file, use the Data tab to update all items.

Excel Worksheet Operations

A worksheet contains various columns and rows. The crossroads of a row and a column are a cell. Different options can be done with a worksheet.

- Insert: This option allows us to insert an existing workbook with a new worksheet.

- Delete: With this option, we can remove selected worksheets from a current workbook.

- Rename: This option permits us to rename the worksheet.

- Move or Copy: This choice enables you to pass or copy a worksheet to a worksheet. You may also adjust the worksheet order with this function.

- View Code: This option lets you view VBA macro code in the worksheet selected.

- Protect Sheet: This choice helps us to lock or secure the worksheet by the password.

- Tab Color: This choice helps us to color the table.

- Hide: This option allows us to hide the worksheet selected from the current workbook.

- Unhide: With this choice, we can activate worksheets in the current workbook.

- Select All Sheets: This option enables us to remove, move, or copy workbooks to a different worksheet.

Change Worksheet Tab Color

In Excel 2019, the use of different tab colors can distinguish various worksheet tabs. If the sheet tabs are color-coded, the sheet tab's name is highlighted in the user-specified color. If the tab shows a background color, the tab has not been selected.

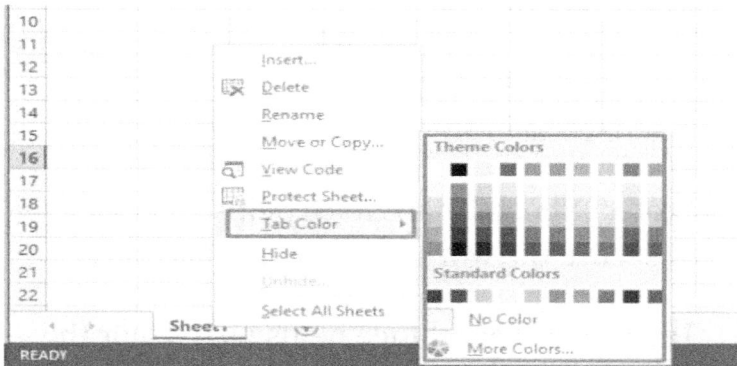

Hide and Unhide Excel Worksheet

Sometimes we may want to hide certain security worksheets and then unhide when necessary. For example, we can conveniently cover the rule data worksheet when building a dashboard for the top management to evaluate. If worksheets are hidden, the formulas do not affect them.

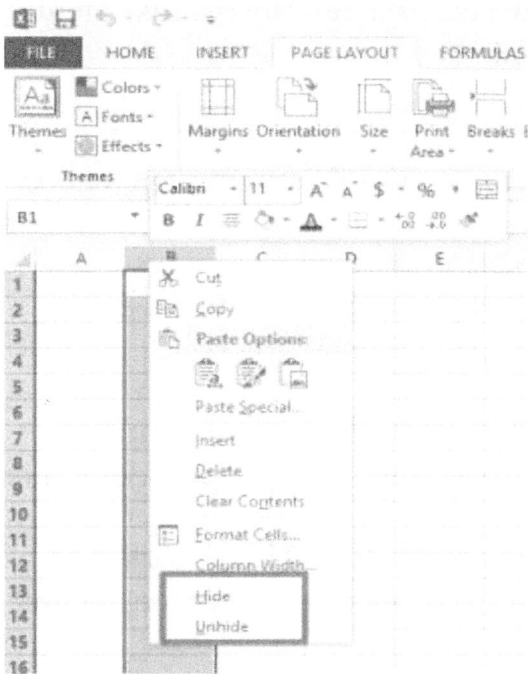

All worksheets can be hidden in a workbook, but at least one worksheet has to be seen.

Business Example

Alex needs to work with multiple worksheets simultaneously to create and collect employee data. Alex needs to use the Color tab and Show / Unhide tools to handle several worksheets.

Here is an overview of Excel's workbook for tab color and hide/unhide.

- Right-click to open the context menu in the worksheet window.

- To change the tab's color, pick the color object from the Tab menu, and choose the color.

- Right-click on the table to cover a worksheet and pick the secret menu.

- Right-click on the table to unhide a worksheet and select an unhidden menu.

- Tap to choose the hidden worksheet and click OK to view the worksheet again.

- Search and Replace Data

Excel 2019 allowed us to search for data and substitute new data for old data. This function is really useful for scanning and removing data in many documents rather than going from cell to cell to alter. This feature saves time and energy as well.

GoTo and Named Box

GoTo and named box functions in Excel can be used to move quickly in a worksheet to different cells. This function is helpful when operating on a wide variety of details.

You may use GoTo and Named Box in a worksheet to pick named cells and a specific data set. The GoTo feature enables us to select all comments, constants, formulas, visible cells, conditional format, and blank cells in a worksheet.

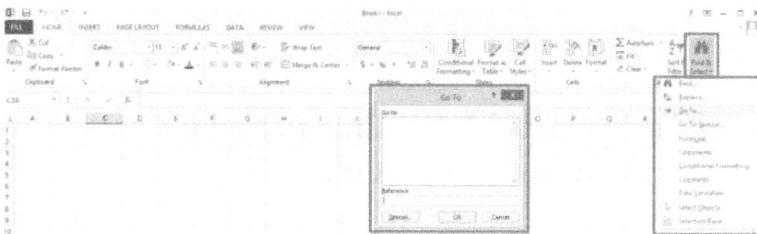

Business Example

Marketing is now renamed the Online Marketing Department. Alex has been tasked with changing this in the datasheet of the employee. He wants to complete this task with the Excel 2019 tool of Find and Replace. Alex must navigate through large worksheets in Excel when managing employee data records. He wants to explore ways to navigate a worksheet like GoTo and Name Box.

Have an overview of the steps for finding and replacing them in Excel.

- Click on the find and select menu in the Home Tab editing group to locate and replace a certain entry in an Excel worksheet.

- Select the Replace item.

- When finding and replacing the pop-up window, type the value in which field to select.

- Select and click the required.txt or.csv file.

- Type in the field the value to replace the current one and click OK.

- Close the find and substitute the pop-up window.

- Choose the GoTo choice in the Find and click the menu to move to a specific row and column.

- In the reference field, type the column and row to jump to and click OK.

Select the reference column first in the GoTo pop-up window to worksheets with a lot of data and then jump to the row using the Name box.

Hyperlinks

Hyperlinks allow fast access via links to other files, documents, and workbooks of Excel. The hyperlinks to the Excel worksheets may be of the following kind:

- **Existing file or Web page:** This alternative lets us hyperlink an existing web page or script. We may also link images, photographs, audio, and other types of files.

- **Place in this document:** This option lets us put a hyperlink in the document. Once the cell has been clicked, it jumps into the hyperlinked cell or worksheet.

- **Create a New Document:** This choice helps us to build new documents when you click on the hyperlinked cell.

- **Email Address:** This option gives us access by clicking on the hyperlink cell to the specified e-mail address to send an e-mail.

Business Example

Alex is preparing for the purchasing department an invoice template. For context, you will connect to a specific site page in the database. This can be done by adding hyperlinks.

See the steps for inserting hyperlinks in Excel. Excel workbook.

- Choose the cell you want to insert a hyperlink.

- Right-click on the cell you have chosen.

- Click on the drop-down menu hyperlink.

- Paste the URL into the hyperlink pop-up window address bar.

- Click OK

- To open the webpage, click on the hyperlink.

A hyperlink to an existing document or a place in the current document can also be established.

Modifying Workbook Theme

In Excel 2019, every workbook uses an office theme by default. The topic of a workbook is an exceptional understanding of colors, fonts, and results. Such subjects are circulated through MS office systems to guarantee the uniformity of all official records. You may search the topics, configure them according to the specifications, or even store the current topic and add it to other workbooks.

This feature allows us to change color and style with a single theme selection. Furthermore, in case any cell, style, and color changes have been made, they have applied automatically throughout the workbook.

Modifying Page Setup

Often a worksheet includes a lot of details or sometimes many maps. If we want to print worksheets or workbooks, we have to adjust the page configuration options first.

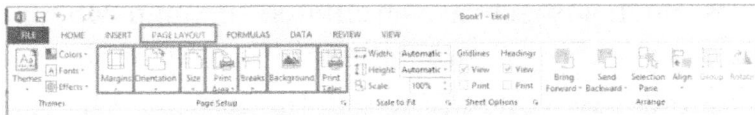

Margins: This option enables us to change or modify the preferences for margins based on our requirements. Some of the options are:

- Default settings or Normal

- Wide and Narrow

Orientation: This choice allows one to alter or adjust the direction of the workbook's style towards a portrait or landscape view.

Size: This option allows us to modify the printing paper size. It also allows us to choose various types of paper sizes.

Print Area: This choice allows us to set an area for printing or clearing prints.

Breaks: This choice helps us to set workbook page breaks.

Backgrounds: With this method, we can set the background to a local or web disk image.

Print Titles: This choice allows us only to print the workbook titles.

Insert and Delete Columns and Rows

We may insert and subtract columns or rows in a worksheet. Columns from A to XFD are labeled, while rows from 1 to 1048576 are labeled.

Below are the shortcut keys for adding and removing columns or rows:

- Shift + SpaceBar: allows the entire row to be picked.

- Control + Spacebar: Allows us to pick the column as a whole.

- Control + or-): (Helps one to choose rows or columns to be omitted from a workbook.

- Shift + control + +: Helps one to insert columns or lines.

- Clear Content Option: allows cell content clearance.

- Change the row height and width of the column

Modify Row Height and Column Width

By design, every section, height, and column width are set to the same measurement in Excel 2019. The height of the row and column width can be changed in various ways, such as text wrap and cell merge.

Often, we have to adjust lines, height, and column manually with cell information displayed clearly or using content automatically. The row height value can be changed from 0 to 249, the value of the column width from 0 to 255.

Hide and Unhide Columns and Rows

At times, we may want to compare certain rows or columns without changing the worksheet structure or temporarily removing a row or column instead of permanently deleting them. Microsoft Excel has a function that lets one cover a row or column from view momentarily.

Business Example

After looking at the employee's data table, John's manager asked him to change the worksheet subject. He also requested that Alex delete the SSN column and insert a new column to add time details for the employees. Alex must also hide the income data when the table appears to others without the column being deleted.

Let's look at the methods used in the Excel workbook to carry out the following activities.

- To modify the topic, click on the page layout tab and select the theme from the themes below.

- To add a section, mark the section to create a new column.

- Right-click on the column you have picked, pick from the contcxt menu with the right-click.

- Select the deleted tab, right-click and press Delete to delete a tab.

- To insert a row, mark a row to insert a new row.

- Right-click on the chosen lines, select Insert from the context menu Right-click.

- Select the deleted row, right-click and click to remove to delete the row to erase a row.

- To cover a column, pick the column you need, right-click and cover.

- To show the column, select the columns on either side of the column, right-click and click Uncloak.

- To hide a row, select the required row, right-click, and click to select.

- To unlock the row, select the above row and the lower row, right-click and click Unhide.

- Pick the line height, press the format, and choose the row height to adjust the row height.

- Type in the required size in the row height pop-up window and click OK.

- Select the section, press format, and press to pick a column width to adjust column width.

- Type into the required size in the pop-up column width window and click OK.

Insert Header and Footers

Microsoft Excel 2019 enables us by adding headers and footers to customize a worksheet. We may add images, page numbers, copyright details, date, time elements, and footers within a worksheet. This information is generally inserted for printing purposes.

Headers and footers are not shown in the worksheet's normal view and are only displayed on page views and printed pages.

Customize Headers and Footers

- Different First Page: This choice makes it possible to discern the first page with a separate header and footer.

- Different Odd and Even Pages: This choice helps us discern headers and footers for odd pages and even posts.

- Scale with Documents: With this choice, we scale the header and footer to suit the text.

- Align with Page Margins: With this option, all document pages can be aligned with printing margins.

Business Example

Alex prepares a purchase department invoice. The date, page number, and business name of every book will be included in the invoice's header and footer.

Let's look at the methods used in the Excel workbook to carry out the following activities.

- Under the Insert tab, press Header and Footer.

- From the template tab, click on the current date.

- Click on the icon for the GoTo footer.

- Click on the Design tab's page number icon.

- Click the Design Tab icon number of pages.

- Tap the button for the GoTo header.

- Click on the first grid and type the text you like. Then press Enter to display the text.

Data Validation

Data validation is an Excel feature, allowing the data entered into a cell to be restricted. By validating data, we can prevent invalid user entry. This task encourages us to enter incorrect data, but it alerts us when we attempt to type it into the cell to determine which data the consumer is allowed to enter.

This feature also includes instructions for users to submit the right entries. Data validation is used mainly to build specific models or workbooks for accurate and reliable data storage for multiple users. When utilizing data authentication, incorrect user entries may be avoided when specified laws below the elevation laws for minimum and average values equal to, respectively, and above.

- Whole number: Users can enter only integers with this method, according to programming software. Whole quantities are referred to as decimal numbers.

- Decimal: This method permits users to only enter decimal values.

- List: This option allows users to view a cell dropdown list of products.

- Date: Users can limit date entries by this method.

- Time: Users can limit time entries with this option.

- Text Length: Users should enter text according to the validation law.

- Custom: This feature helps users to modify options to build a validation law utilizing formulas or functions.

Warning Messages for Data Validation

Data Validation displays users' default inputs and warnings. An input to guide users about the type of data to be entered in cells. This message is shown within the door. When the users enter invalid data, there are three types of error alert messages:

- Stop: This message prohibits users from inserting incorrect data into a cell with two choices. Re-edit or cancel the invalid entry to delete the invalid entry.

- Warning: This warning alarms or informs users whether there are three alternatives to an incorrect request.

  - Yes - to accept the invalid entry

  - No - To edit the invalid entry

  - Cancel - To remove the invalid entry

- Information: This notification alerts users when there are two choices for an invalid request.

  - OK - To accept the invalid value

  - Cancel - To remove the invalid entry

Business Example

Alex gathers new employee information in his business. He wants to restrict the data that will be inserted in a cell to the appropriate information. It is done by Alex using the data validation method.

Let's look at the methods used in the Excel workbook to carry out the following activities.

- Select a cell and click on the data validation tab.

- Pick from the combo box text frequency.

- Select Equal to, from the data combo box, type the limit in the length box, and click OK.

- Pick a cell to configure the input message and click on the data validation page.

- Click the Data Validation input request tab and sort messages.

- To customize error alert messages, click the Error Alert tab, and enter the message.

- Select a warning from the style combo box.

- Click OK.

Enable Developer Tab

Although the Developer tab is not enabled in Excel 2019 by default, we do need to set it to use the following functions:

Write macros in the basic visual editor for tasks automation. Run macros that have been recorded or written before. To work with XML data, use XML commands. Insert and use the form and controls Active X. Create Microsoft office program applications.

Macron Security Options

When opening a workbook, the macro protection settings may be modified to monitor which macro to run and under what circumstances. There are many choices for macro security:

- Deactivate all macros without notification: if set by default, all macros and security alerts in the document are disabled.

- Unable to note macros: When the default is set, macros in the text will be disabled, and the security warning will be alerted.

- Deactivate all macros except digitally signed macros: Unless configured by design, all macros in this document except the digitally signed macros and the security alert would be deactivated without notice. This feature is identical to deactivating all notification option macros.

- Allow all macros: Not advised to run potentially unsafe code. Once this is the case, all macros in the code are operating without any warnings.

- Confidence Access to the VBA Application object model: By default, the project object model includes a protection code that can dynamically optimize an office system and programmatically modify the visual framework base, the VBA configuration, and the object models Microsoft.

Record a Macros

Macros are a set of Excel instructions to automate tasks in a specific worksheet by simply clicking a button. A micro recorder documents the required measures to complete the operation that we want to complete the macro.

This step can include text or numbers, clicking on the ribbon or menu, formatting, cell selection, rows or columns, and mouse dragging to select cells in the worksheet.

- Macro Name: Key a macro name and obey the rules below to set the macros name.

    o Rule 1: the macro name should not have two names.

    o Rule 2: Do not use the application of built-in keywords for the macro name.

o Rule 3: No special characters, symbols, and numeric should begin a macro name.

- Assign Shortcut Keys: You should delegate shortcut keys, the macro, as needed, but it is not mandatory.

- Store Macro: Macros are saved by default in the workbook where we record or write code. If you want to store macros in a new workbook, you must change this option and select a macro workbook for personal use if you want to run macros in all workbooks.

- Description: For each micro, we can give a description to help other users understand the macro, but it's not compulsory.

Business Example

Alex was given a job in an Excel workbook to illustrate the accounting department's profits. In addition to the details of the employees, he wants to explore the macro details.

Let's look at the methods used in the Excel workbook to carry out the following activities.

- Click the options item in the File tab.

- Click the customize ribbon.

- Select the Developer check box to add the Developer tab to the ribbon and click OK.

- Click macro security on the Developer tab.

- Choose to enable the (") option for all macros (not suggested; potentially dangerous code can run), and click OK.

- On the Developer tab, click Record macro item. Right-click the selected lines, pick Select from the context menu with the right-click.

- Enter the required information in the pop-up record macro pane.

- Perform the tasks in the macro that are to be registered.

- Press the item to avoid recording.

- Click on the Display tab for macros.

- Choose view macros.

- Pick this macro workbook in.

- Select the macro name.

- Press Execute.

Backward Compatibility

Backward compatibility implies testing compliance with new or existing versions of the same commodity. A new version of the programmer, if it uses files and data created in an older version from the same program, is backward compatible. Backward compatibility is critical since data can be readily shared and retrieved irrespective of the Excel edition in use.

Typically speaking, producers seek to maintain quality with all their goods. But we sometimes have to sacrifice the feature of backward compatibility in every product to benefit from new technology. In Excel 2019, we will test the backward compatibility in three ways with previous versions.

- Inspect Document: This choice helps you search for the workbook's secret property or your details.

- Check Accessibility: This option allows us to check the accessibility to disabled people of the workbook content.

- Check Compatibility: This choice allows it easy to test the workbook functionality's consistency with previous Excel models.

Excel apps have no backward compatibility, ensuring that the current Excel function releases cannot be included with prior Excel models.

Workbook Views

In Excel 2019, workbook views are assumed to be natural by default, and we often need to adapt according to the requirements. The Excel application contains four workbook view types.

- Normal: Displays the ruler and allows data to enter the cells to insert graphs and images.

- Page Break View: Shows a page breaks workbook and page numbers to adjust the work with the print content.

- Page Layout: Displays a workbook as ruler pages, headers, and footers are displayed. It is mainly used for printing.

- Custom View: Allows us to change workbooks use customized zoom choices.

Once this option is set and the workbook is opened, it automatically zooms in the world book as specified.

Zoom for Excel Workbooks

We may use the zoom feature if the workbook contains huge data and does not display all the window content. We can zoom in and zoom out with a camera to increase a camera viewing object size. In the lower right corner, next to the workbook view icons, is the zoom function.

Zoom Out: To decrease workbook, zoom-size, and minimum zoom-level of 10%, click on this option.

Zoom In: To increasing the workbook zoom size and maximum zoom level, click this link.

Freeze Panes

Occasionally, when our workbook includes a lot of material, and it is challenging to evaluate pieces, in Excel 2019, we have an alternative called freeze pains.

- Freeze Panes: That choice causes the rows and columns to remain clear for the others, depending on the existing layout of the worksheet, except when going up and down.

- Freeze Top Row: This option allows the highest row's visibility and is preferred when the highway has headers.

- Freeze First Column: This choice provides clarity for the first column and is favored if headers are in the first column.

Click the Freeze Panes command to unfreeze the rows or columns, and select Unfreeze Panes from the drop-down menu.

Split Window

Occasionally, we can have to review various parts of the same workbook without a fresh browser. For these instances, the separated window feature may be included. This command helps us, scroll bars and increase or decrease the window size, to split the worksheet into four sections.

Business Scenarios

Alex works with a lot of Excel info. You need to swipe down to display data lines, so as you hit the bottom of the page, the column will vanish in the top half. The whole data sheet may not be displayed from left to right. He needs to use freeze panes and break window functionality in Excel 2019 to display all datasheets.

Let's look at the methods used in the Excel workbook to carry out the following activities.

- Click the View tab to freeze a row or column.

- In the windows category, press freeze panes objects.

- Click on the top row freeze or freeze the first column item.

- To unblock a row or column, press to unblock the panes from the freezer screen.

- To divide the display into separate windows, press the Divide button on the Display page.

- To remove the dissection, click split again.

Show Formulas

In Excel, we can see formula results in cells by default, and sometimes we need to see which cells contain formulas. When utilizing the view formulas function, the procedures can be shown in both cells instead of the formulation product. This functionality allows us to interpret all formulas easily to test for errors.

Business Example 1

The HR department submitted a report on the profits to John. The model used was tested, and estimates were confirmed.

- Let us look at the measures used in the Excel workbook to carry out the above tasks.

- Select the cell to be presented with the formula.

- Select and check the Formulas on the Formulas page.

- Add Excel Workbook Assets Values.

By default, the name of the person who created the workbook in Excel 2019 is the workbook author. Nevertheless, a workbook may also include many writers, including the names of each author in the workbook.

We can attach additional writer info, such as title, tanks and comments, rank, subject type, name of the base company hyperlink, and the author's manager.

Business Example 2

The HR department gave John an employee survey. He was told to apply a title and tag to the workbook to allow arranging and recalling the workbook simpler.

Let's look at the methods used in the Excel workbook to carry out the following activities.

Click the file tab.

- Type correct entries in the text boxes with titles and tags.

- Click on all properties to display the entire properties of the workbook.

- Save workbooks in alternate file formats.

In Excel 2019, by example, workbooks will be saved with XLXS file extension, and we can save a workbook in alternative file formats, as mentioned below.

XPS: Specification of XML paper: Helps one to print a workbook quickly. For instance, if we haven't had access to the printer and anyone else, however, they haven't had Excel built on their machine; we are rescuing this file format.

Text(txt): Saves a workbook |as a tab-bound text file—the most widely compatible text files for data. You cannot open and view them on any computer. Typically, they are called.txt scripts.

Comma Separated Values (CSV): Saves a workbook as a text file delimited by a comma. Comma-separated value files are a category of a text file that does not store formatting details, as in the original table. Usually, they are called. CSV files.

Set the Print Area for an Excel Workbook

We need to print often a worksheet that contains a ton of details. Excel helps one to configure the print region in this situation. This option enables us to set a print area according to our needs and clear the print area if necessary.

Three ways to print workbooks:

- Prince Active Sheets: This choice allows us only to print active content for worksheets.

- Print Entire Workbook: This choice allows us to print the whole content of the workbook.

- Print Selection: This choice helps us only to print the selected worksheet region. A worksheet Prince region can be submitted in page split view mode.

Business Example

After looking at the employee data chart, the director asked John to print the columns employee code, last name, first name, SSN, and zone. Alex wants to print the prince's field. Let's look at the methods used in the Excel workbook to carry out the following activities.

- Select the columns/area for printing.

- Click the Layout tab of the page and press the element on the print section.

- Select the print area menu element from the drop-down display.

- To continue, press OK.

- Click on the File tab and click print.

- Click on the button for printing.

- Click the black arrow to go back to clear the print area.

- Press again on the item in the print section.

- Click on the menu item for the transparent print area.

Save Workbooks to Remote Location

We have many ways to exchange workbooks online in Excel 2019. We can save that the cloud file, publish a link, share the file via various social media platforms, or email it. Excel files can be stored on the cloud and linked to SkyDrive Windows.

SkyDrive is a Microsoft-hosted cloud storage facility. The advantages of utilizing the cloud space are that we can access the data from everywhere and every computer. But only if we have a Microsoft account will we use SkyDrive.

Notes:

Let's sum up what we have learned so far.

- MS Excel Workbook is a tab that can be entered and processed in the MS Excel program. An existing workbook or a blank document can be used to create a workbook.

- Macros are a set of Excel instructions to automate tasks in a specific worksheet by simply clicking a button.

- Macros are a series of rules or guidance for Excel to simplify activities completed with a single click of a button on a specific worksheet.

- Excel worksheets may be housed in the formats .pdf,.txt, and.csv. This feature ensures consistency with other operating systems.

- SkyDrive is an MS program that requires data to be downloaded electronically from anywhere.

UNDERSTANDING YOUR MAIN SCREEN PAGE

You will see a simple screen when you first open Excel in Office or a modern Microsoft Office version. From this view, these are the key features:

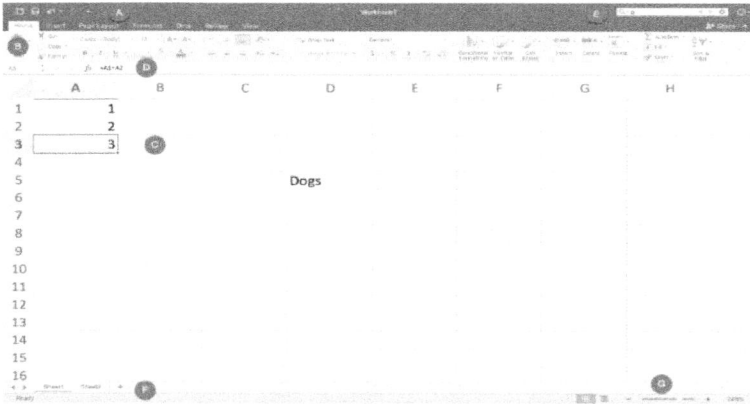

A. Simple App Functions: From the left to the right, icons should be displayed around the top green banner: restart the Build a Workbook tab, save your work, redo the last activity performed to display which activity was reported, redo an ineffective move, pick which resources to use in the following area.

B. Ribbon: This gray region is called the ribbon and includes data entry, editing, and visualization software. There are also pages based on different characteristics. Click on the Insert, Page Layout, Formula, Data, Review, or View tab to reveal a set of unique tools to each tab. This will be discussed later in the section "Navigating the Ribbon."

C. Spreadsheet Work Area: The job environment is a grid by nature. The column headers A through Z (and beyond) are at the tip, and the row headers are listed on the left side. The increasing rectangle of the table is called a cell and is identified by column letter and row number. For example, the selected cell is A3.

D. Formula Bar: The Formula Bar shows details in a single marked cell or cell set. If you have entered "1" as a number in cell A1, "1" is seen in the Formula Column. In Formula Row, the simple text you insert in a cell always exists.

In Formula Bar, there are situations where what you see is different than what is in the container. Let's assume, for starters, A1 = 1 and A2 = 2. If you build a formula in A3 that is A1 + A2, then your cell will represent "3" in your worksheet, but the formula bar will indicate "= A1 + A2," so this is crucial as you want to transfer cells into certain areas in your worksheet.

That said, the actual cell meaning is taken into consideration by certain calculations that relate a cell. If $A4 = A3 + 1$, it will be equivalent to 4, since it stacks the A3 (A1 + A2) structure with $A4 = A3 + 1$. Formulas may frequently reference other formulas.

E. Search Bar: The only key in the value to show all cells that hold this value. It must not be an exact match. For example, you would find a cell labeled "Dogs" among your search results if you looked for "o."

F. Sheet Tabs: This is where you can locate the various sheets in your workbook. Every sheet has its tab that you can call. This may be useful for splitting data to prevent crushing one layer.

For example, you might provide an overall budget with a column per month, and a form of the cost could section. Instead of monitoring and horizontal scrolling each year on one board, you can render a separate year of just 12 months in each column.

Please note that data from different sheets may be retrieved in the same workbook for formulas. For example, you might bring Sheet2 data into Sheet1 with two sheets, Sheet1 and Sheet2.

If you had the cell A1 in sheet 1 equivalent to the cell A1 in sheet 2, you should place the formula in A1: "= sheet2! A1. "A1." The exclamation mark calls the previous page until the data is found.

G. Viewability Options: The left icon is Standard. The right icon is Page Layout, which separates the worksheet into pages that mimic the way it appears when written, including headers. The-" "and" + "slider on it is for scale or zoom level. Drag and lower the lever to zoom in or out.

Navigating the Ribbon

The home tab is where you handle the sheet design and presentation, along with a few basic formulas that you still have to use.

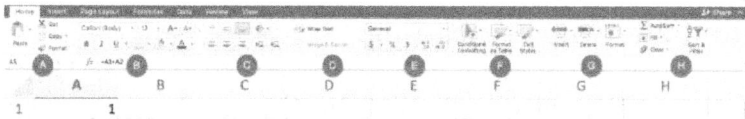

A. Tools to copy and paste: Use these tools to duplicate data and format styles in the table rapidly. The device Copy may either copy a specified cell or group of cells or copy the region of your tablet in another document like a photograph. The Cut method transfers cell collection to a different target instead of duplicating it.

The Paste method will insert something into the chosen cell in your clipboard and usually preserves all the meanings, formulas, and formats. However, Excel has a range of suitable options: you can find them by clicking on the down arrow above the suit icon.

You should paste as an image of what you copied. You may even paste what you copied as values just to twice the final value seen in the cell instead of duplicating a copied cell function.

The paintbrush format copies all the formats relevant to the selected container. By choosing a cell and clicking on the format, a whole set of cells may be displayed, and each cell takes formatting without altering its meaning.

B. Visual Formatting Tools: Some of these resources are identical to Microsoft Word. To adjust the font, size, and color of typed words, you use the formatting software to render them bold, italicized or highlighted. It also has a few table layout choices.

You may select which cell sides and their design and thickness are additional boundaries. The highlight color of the entire cell can also be modified. It is useful to build visually pleasing boundaries or separate columns or highlight a particular cell that you want to accentuate.

C. Position Formatting Tools: Align cell data upwards, downwards, or halfway across the loop. There is also an alternative to add the shown values, which will make reading easier. On the lower side, the left, middle, and right orientation choices are common. There are both left and right keys.

D. Multi-cell Formatting Features: This segment includes two main features that address new Excel users' typical problems. The first is the text of the seal. Normally, it spills into the next cell if the text is inserted in a cell that is beyond the cell size. For example, if you type "Cheap products" into A1, some of the term "Cheap items" flows into B1. Then if you click B1, all the A1 characters that have been added to B1 are protected.

The additional cell A1 text remains, but it is now concealed. Tap on the Wrap Text button on A1 if you don't want to stretch cells - this split 'Cashed products' into two packed lines rather than one in A1. This makes the whole row larger for the text.

Form B1 does not protect the current text anymore.

Merge, and Center is the other method in this segment. Sometimes you may want to combine multiple cells and have them function as one long cell. You might want a header to be clear and easy to read for an entire table for starters.

Choose all the cells that you want, press Combine and then enter and shape your header. While the default header configuration is based text, just press the down arrow to choose numerous fusion and evolving choices.

E. Numbers-based Format Settings: A drop-down panel includes numerical formatting options. For instance, currency places everything you want in "$0.00" format and transforms percent to "50 percent" (date).

These are simple format choices, but more types may be chosen from the menu below, to achieve more advanced uses (different currencies of nations, or the configuration of "(xxx)xxx-xxxx" throughout the number sequence). Sometimes, you may use these methods to hold all data in one group the same way on entire columns.

F. Table or Sheet Formatting: Grid and cell style may be used with templates or tables (e.g., contrasting row colors and outlined header bars). Pick your data set and select a formatting type.

Conditional formatting is a bit more difficult. You may choose from various choices using the drop-down menu, such as adding helpful visual symbols reflecting rank or ending, or adjusting the colors of various ranks.

The conditional rules that are generated with a basic logic are most essential. For instance, let's assume you have a column with A1 to A3 details, and A4 contains the total of those three columns. You might put formatting on A4 with one rule, stating that if A4 >0, then highlight A4 green, attach another rule that says "if A4 < 0, then color A4 red." Now, you have an easy visual reference where green = a positive number and red = a negative number that will adjust depending on what you enter in A1, A2, and A3. A4 has a simple visual reference.

G. Row and Column Formatting Tools: Throughout the Select Drop Down button, lines, rows, or columns are put on the sheet before or after a specified field and are deleted. The Dropdown Format helps you to adjust the row height and column width. They also have ways to mask those parts and unhide them.

H. Miscellaneous Tools: From the top left, AutoSum allows you to select a swath of cells and place a sum in the cell directly below or to the right of the last data point selected. You can use the dropdown to modify the average function, display the maximum, minimum, or count of selected numbers.

Use Fill to take a cell's contents and expand them to as many cells as you want. When the cell has a name, Fill would automatically repeatedly copy the name. Whether it includes a formula, the relative location for every new cell should be recalculated. If the first cell is equal to A1+B1, the next cell will be equivalent to A2+B2, etc.

You may clear the meaning or even plain cell layout with the Plain click.

The Sort & Filter tools help you to select what and in which order to view. This method classifies cells with text from A to Z and cells with lower to higher numbers at the base level. This can also be ordered with color or symbol. Sorting and filtering only helps the data you need to surface.

Use the Add feature to incorporate extra items that go beyond text and colors to the Excel workbook:

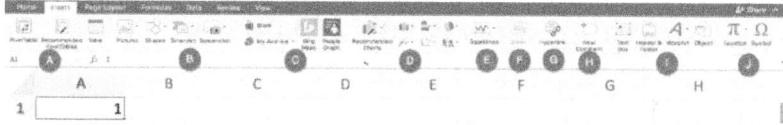

A. Such tools monitor the essential Excel feature PivotTables. Think of PivotTables as "files" for easy visualization of all the results, review of patterns, and findings. You will easily create a visually pleasing table by choosing at least two rows of data and by clicking on the PivotTable.

Through the method, the PivotTable Builder continues to help you pick columns to use, sort, and drag and drop them into the table easily. You should have collapsible rows for immersive and uncluttered files. There's even a PivotTables click that can support if you don't know where to go.

The table creates a plain table that comprises whatever amount of columns you choose. This transforms data into a table on the location, rather than the table somewhere on the worksheet, and adds unique color formats.

B. You may insert visual elements such as picture files, preconstructed shapes, and SmartArt in this portion. You can add forms, resize them, and color them again to create intuitive data sets and reports. SmartArt artifacts are pre-built diagrams in which text and knowledge may be embedded. They are great to show what the data says elsewhere on your workbook.

C. These devices are used for adding objects from other Microsoft goods, such as Bing Charts, pre-built People Identification Cards, and add-ins from your shop.

D. To create diagrams and graphs, use these tools. Most of them work only if one or more data sets are selected (only numbers, with words for headers or categories).

Charts and charts function as you would expect – just select the data you want to view, and select the type of visual you want to see (bar charts, dispersion plots, pie charts, or line diagrams). To build one, you can create formatting choices to change color, labels, and more.

E. Sparklines are simplified graphs that can accommodate as little as a node. For a simple, small visual representation, you can position them next to the results.

F. Slicers are broad sets of buttons that increase the interactiveness of the results. The PivotTable you've built can be selected, and then a slicer developed-enabling a viewer to click on buttons that correspond with the data they want to filter.

G. You may build a cell or table in a clickable page by using this hyperlink method. If an audience clicks on the cell(s), it will be brought to whatever web portal or intranet link you choose.

H. Recent Excel versions allow greater cooperation — insert statement to add more significance to either cell or smartphone spectrum. To stop so much confusion in the worksheet, you can allow or close comments.

I. A text box helps make a report when you don't want to use written terms like cells. It makes moving your text easy, rather than cutting and pasting cells (which could damage real data).

The next field is for Headers & Footers, where you can apply headers and footers for the entire website. The website view. On the other hand, WordArt allows you to embellish the text. Insert Object allows you to insert entire files into the worksheet (Word documents, PDFs, etc.).

J. You may insert equations and symbols in this portion. Using calculations to compose a statistical equivalent with percentages, variables, and more can be put like a text box in your board. It may be useful to illustrate how a section of a table has been measured in a study of starters. Symbols, on the other hand, can be directly inserted into the cells and contain all non-standard characters from both most languages and emojis.

The Page Layout tab contains everything to change your worksheet's structural parts, especially for printing or presentation purposes:

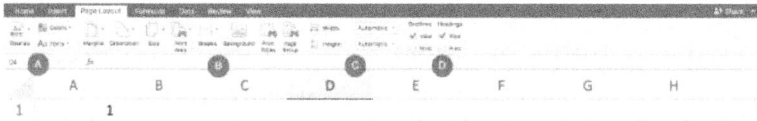

A. Use these buttons to adjust the whole sheet's visual style quickly. You can control fonts and colors and use the Themes section to add them easily for clean and well-designed sheets for each screen, PivotTable, and SmartArt feature.

B. There are choices for printing. Whether you want a vertical or horizontal orientation, the cells in your book you want to print, where you want page breaks, or if there is a context (for instance, to insert the business name), you will change the margin for printing.

You can also use the Print Titles button to begin to indicate a heading for each page and the order to print each section.

C. This helps you to pick how many articles you would like to print and how many articles.

D. This segment helps you to choose how the automated grids exist for the sheet work and the row and column headings to be printed (A, B, C, 1, 2, 3, etc.).

The Formulas tab avoids almost all that contributes to Excel's prestige as a "hard" as this segment is intended for beginners:

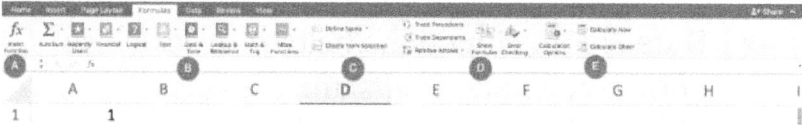

A. For those who don't know all shorthand, the Insert Function button is useful. This brings up a side section for Formula Creator explaining each feature so you can pick the one to use.

B. All roles are separated by category by these keys.

- AutoSum works in the same way as the Home tab does.

- Recently used, frequently used formulas are useful for saving time looking at menus.

- Financial covers all currencies, prices, depreciation, yields, rate, and more.

- Logical functions provide conditional functions, such as "IF X THEN Y."

- Text functions aid in cleaning, modifying, and evaluating plain text cells such as cell count view (helpful for posts on Twitter), merging the two separate rows using Concatenate, or delete numeric meaning from non-formatted data entries.

- Date & Time functions help to make sense of time-formatted cells and include "TODAY" entries that reach the current day.

- Lookup & Index functions allow you to pull details from various sections of your workbook to avoid the quest difficulty.

- Math & Trig functions are exactly as they sound like and require all sorts of mathematical practice.

- More Functions include Statistical and Engineering data.

C. This segment includes choices for marking. When you also need to refer to a set of cells or a table in formulae, you can describe its name and add it here. For starters, assume that you have a column with the entire list of items you are selling. You can highlight the names in that list and define the name as a "ProductList." You can simply type "ProductList" every time that you want to refer to this column in a form (instead of finding that data collection once again or storing their cell positions).

D. It includes methods for error reporting. Trace Precedents and Trace Dependents help you see which cells comprise formulas that apply to a specific cell and vice versa. The Formula shows formulas, not their display values, within all cells. Error Checking finds broken links and other problems with your tablet.

E. You will use this segment to start calculations and even select which category of data will not operate because you have a wide sheet with a large number of linked formulas, tables, and cells.

The Data tab is used to evaluate more complex data than most beginners require:

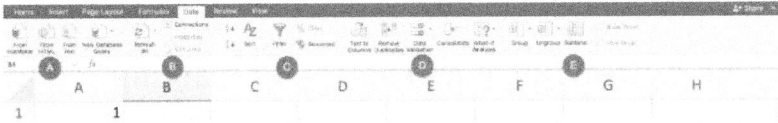

A. They are resources for importing computer data from either site, file, or cloud computer.

B. This segment allows you to repair database relations, update data, and change properties.

C. These are similar Sort and Filter options to those used in data feed on your sheet. They are particularly important here, as a database surely has more information than you can or care to use.

D. Those are methods for computer engineering. You may take a single long line, such as commas or spaces divided from each other, and split it into columns with Column Text.

You will look for and delete duplicates, merge cells, and test if data follow those requirements to determine their accuracy. When research allows you to address missing data holes, use current evidence and patterns to predict possible outcomes for different scenarios.

E. These tools help you manage the amount of data you need to handle at once and group it according to any criteria you consider necessary. It's like sorting, except you can pick any number of columns or rows and fall, each with its name. Using Subtotal to make automated estimates according to a variety of details, useful for financial papers.

The Test tab is in the Ribbon, which helps to share and check accuracy:

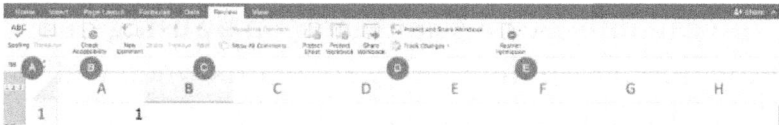

A. These are basic text-based tests (like Word), which allow you to spot cells with errors in spelling or find more appropriate terms with the Thesaurus.

B. Accessibility check retrieves errors which may make access to data in other programs difficult or for reading purposes only. You may find that your sheet lacks alt text or that you use defaults on sheet names that can make navigation less intuitive.

C. The commenting resources encourage workers to "talk" inside the board.

D. Protection and communication tools allow you to invite workers and restrict access to other board parts. You can delegate different access rates individually; for example, you can authorize a worker to change only cells relevant to the hours they operate, but not cells that measure their compensation.

Unlike Text, posting a sheet with Tracked Changes ensures that you will display everything that has been completed.

E. You can limit permissions later on by using this button and pick individual participants when you have shared a workbook.

Using the Display tab software to adjust configurations on what you will see or do:

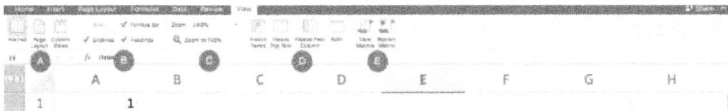

A. It is your simple view of how the default sheet image should appear as you print, and how you set up. That is the specific display.

B. To display the charts, headings, screen bar, and ruler, use these keys.

C. This is another way that zooms in and out of cells are regulated.

D. Freeze Pane controls are an essential aspect of a functional console. You will freeze a selection of rows and/or columns when flipping around using these devices. Of instance, if the first row has all of the headings of your column and stayed frozen, you already know which column to look at as to scroll down.

E. Macros are a way to automate Excel processes. Nonetheless, it is well above Excel 101.

FORMULA BAR

Also defined as a formula window, a formula bar is a Microsoft Excel segment and other table applications. It displays the current cell contents and allows you to create and view formulas. The following two images demonstrate how the formulation bar appears in Microsoft Excel. Select the cursor in the formula bar to continue generating formula and insert the same symbol (=). We use the = SUM in the examples below, which informs Excel to include each cell.

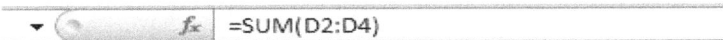

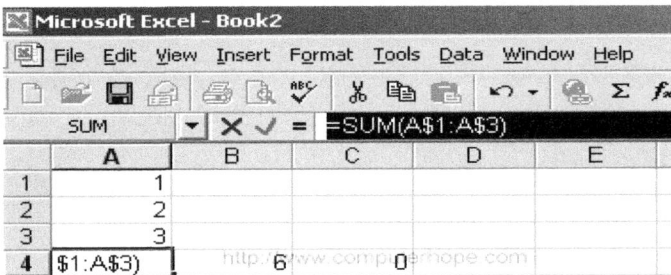

Where Is the Formula Bar Located in Microsoft Excel?

The formula bar is placed immediately above the table for table-top applications such as Microsoft Excel, as seen in the next image.

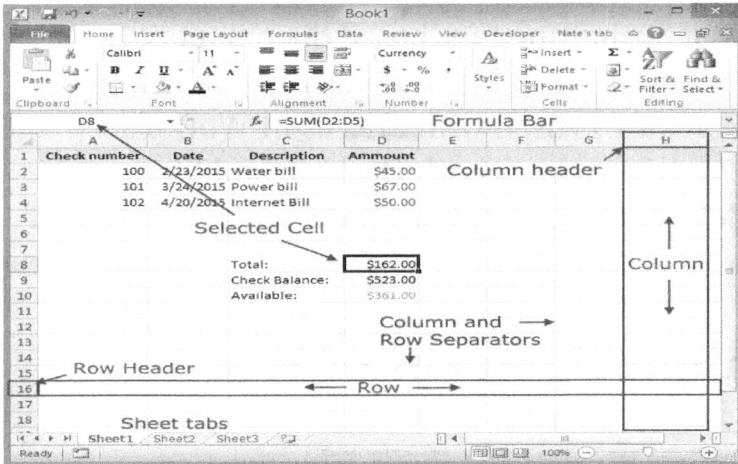

The formula bar has above a "= SUM(D2: D5)" cell material that adds values in column D in lines 2, 3, 4, 5. The result in this table is $162.00. Cell D5 is empty and is considered nil.

HOW TO CREATE A SPREADSHEET IN WORD?

Study all the fundamentals for a Microsoft Word table. Word is the most popular word processing application in the world and offers numerous ways of formatting text-based documents, including simple tables and tablets. Like Excel, the software is used with Microsoft Workplace and Mobile and has both Desktop and Mac models. Each chapter uses the Standard edition of Microsoft Word.

Unique Features of Word

However, Word is not just a table program, rather a framework for the form and arrangement of text papers. This is much simpler to structure Word sentences or paragraphs than in Excel text frames, let alone in containers. Word can, therefore, be used to create compelling reports or to insert half-workable data, for example, an article, into a heavy text document.

Word has two options to build a tablet: to construct basic tables in the software or to incorporate Excel sheets and maps.

Understanding the Word Interface

Contrary to Excel, where everything in the ribbon is critical for making a notebook, only a few Word things are significant. For example, almost all you need is included in the Insert page. Here are the corresponding tools for the insert tab:

A. Table: To create basic tables in a few ways, click this button. When you click Table, the grid will appear and click to select the number of vertical and horizontal cells for your table. If you press Insert Row, you get a pop-up window that lets you define the row's measurements by clicking the number of columns and lines in the table and specifying the cell width.

Eventually, you may pick a Draw Table to move and create as many cells as you like. Although it seems obvious, Draw table is not necessarily the cheapest or simplest way to construct a Word table.

B. Chart: When you click on this icon, a drop-down menu appears with the same sizes and styles of maps, with the same interface, as Excel. You're likely to use scatter maps, pie charts, line diagrams, etc.

C. Table Design and Layout: When you click on every table in your Word document, the middle of the ribbon — Table Arrangement and Configuration — includes two additional tabs. All tabs function for tables only and include the Ribbon menus listed below.

D. Object: You will explicitly put Excel things into your Word paper. Either attach a Microsoft Excel Map or a Worksheet from Microsoft Excel. If you select any of these options, Excel will open to create and edit a fully-functional table, which will then appear as it stands in the Word document.

The tablets and maps are like icons in Word so that you can transfer and rotate them and even double-click them to open Excel and change their details.

An unused Excel tab may also be added. Click From File to do this, then navigate to the Excel file location and open it. At first, just the primary sheet shows, but double-click it to allow others to view the workbook in its entirety unless you cover it.

Let's focus on the Design Table tab. Such solutions are available for Word-based tables, not Excel tables.

E. Use these toggles to select certain items in the table layout like column, row, or header.

F. They are somewhat similar types to Excel table models, with a wide variety of colors and variations. Additionally, you should customize the lighting with the paint bucket icon instead of choosing one from the drop-down screen.

G. Such tools help you to plan the boundaries of every cell and the whole array. Thickness, color, and line form (dotted, smooth, wavy, etc.) can be selected.

Let's see the Design category next. Again, this works only for Word generated tables

H. Using such methods to pick rows and choose whether or not grid lines are shown. You can also open the properties window and edit different elements, table alignment, or the boundaries and shades.

I. This is another location for the table drawing and erasing devices. Use these tools to move your mouse and draw each cell one side at a time and delete it.

J. These are rows, columns, or whole tables deletion tools. You may also do this by clicking on a file, right-clicking, and removing these parts.

K. Insert rows or columns with these tools wherever you want in your table. Again, by highlighting and right-clicking the different parts of the table, you can access these tools.

L. These tools help you to modify your table organization. As in Excel, you can unite and unbundle cells. This is a helpful function to construct headers or to split the list. You may also split the table into two sides.

M. Autofit to fit the table automatically into the Word document's room or make every column the same distance.

N. Choose rows and columns' height and width numerically instead of utilizing drag and fall.

O. Using these methods to pick several rows or columns and uniformly spread them across the page to render the table smooth and tidy.

P. The alignment software can help you decide how each cell (top left, bottom right, middle, etc.) should be balanced.

Q. This is, therefore, possible to select whether the document is horizontal or vertical.

R. Here's where the simple table functions work, although they aren't as powerful as Excel. Select operates the same way, enabling you to pick several rows in a column to alphabetize the list. Convert to Text enables you to select any number of cells and put them in a table-free text without commas or spaces. This can be helpful for subsequent content editing or importing data into other applications.

Finally, the roles are there. Word tables have 18 core features, primarily quantitative, and some conceptual features Now and THEN. Calling cells of formulas of Word is quite a little harder. Every cell is row 1-A1, B1, C1, etc. if you have a single row chart.

These aren't numbered, though, so you only have to count or memorize them. If you want to know the sum of all cells of a column and put it in the last cell, you can also call by position and then select the last cell and make the form "= SUM (abode)" as well.

The map feature is the other important thing for tablets that can be produced in Term. Click the Insert Chart button in the Insert tab to access this function. Once you have selected a template, it opens Excel to edit the chart details. Yet if the table is in Html, instead of the Table Layout and Layout, there are two additional Ribbon lines.

They are the template and style of the map.

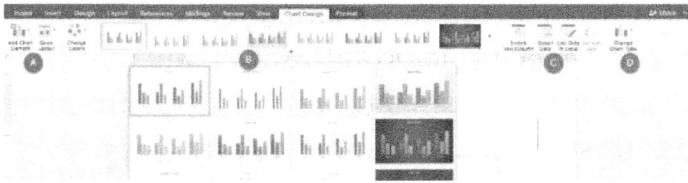

A. Using such methods, either individually with Add Map Elements or use the handy templates for Fast Design, to attach extra critical elements to your table.

B. Using these methods to adjust the graphic type without too much alteration in shape. You can adjust shades, decrease shadows, backdrop, etc.

C. Manipulate data using this collection of methods in the table. Turn Row / Column allows you to change your chart's X-Y axes. Select Data should drive you right into your Excel session to select the data collection you like in the table.

Excel Edit Data lets you adjust everything you want about Excel info. Double-clicking on your map will even take you to Excel. Click Refresh Data when you return to Word to update your diagram to reflect any Excel data changes.

D. Switch Chart Style enables you to turn to a line chart with the same data collection.

See the Layout tab now.

E. The app helps you to pick which section of the map you'd like to modify so that you don't press somewhere inadvertently. The Plot region where the graph is held, the Diagram region where all axis labels occur, and every other dimension can be chosen.

F. Using this to insert forms on the table, much like every other entity is placed into Phrase.

G. Using such methods to color each item in your map could involve how lines, text color, and more are filled in.

H. Use these resources to color anything on your map that may include filling in curves, the color of the document, and more.

I. Similar to positioning certain items in Phrase, the positioning tools function. You can wrap the text around the chart with the wrap text and position it on the page behind or in front of any other element.

J. Use these tools to change the height and width of the whole chart numerically. The map's height and width may also be changed by picking the corner or side and changing it with the cursor.

K. This unlocks the Style Window, with some of the same Ribbon devices, except it's bigger and simpler to use for others.

How to Import a Spreadsheet and Chart into Word from Excel?

Now that you have heard about the Word tablet software, you can use many different forms to translate a current tablet into Term.

Step 1: Create a Word Document

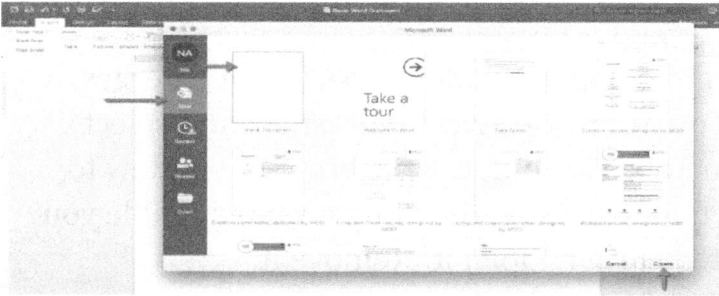

This screen appears when you open the Term. The New Register on the page helps you to build a new document, newly updated pages, Sharing displays documents submitted to you from other Word users, and Open opens a file explorer to access a current document.

In the New tab, you can see several templates you can use to directly produce various types of documents, such as abstracts, blogs, and research papers. Most may not apply to tablets, so press On Blank Paper at the top left corner.

Step 2: Save Your Document

After your document has been developed, save it, and pick a place to store it by clicking on the store icon above. Offer it a name that is important to it, so it is simple to locate.

Step 3: Import an Excel Workbook into Your Document

When the popup window Insert Item emerges, click on Microsoft Excel Worksheet and select From Tab. This opens a file browser window to select, for example, the Simple Budget Table you created earlier. Open it. Remove it.

Step 4: Resize Spreadsheet to Fit

A table as big as the one we have produced is too wide for a standard Word document. To minimize it, after you have tapped on the imported list, keep down the Shift key.

When pressing Move, pick an edge of the table and drag it several times to the piece's middle. It is important to note that tablets act as a regular image or object in Word so that you can drag and resize them as you wish. Feel free to apply the text below the chart.

Regardless of the size of the monitor, you cannot communicate with Word info. Both the methods and designs must still stay unchanged. You will also interact for most of the text, type terms, and place photos across the page.

Step 5: Edit the Data in Excel

Double-click the table to open the table in a new Excel window to modify info. You can modify some data here. It changes in real-time so that the adjustment can be mirrored in Word after your adjustment Excel. In this way, you will directly put completely functioning tablets into Term.

Note: Double-clicking on an embedded element like an Excel workbook allows you access to the entire workbook, not just the first book displayed in Word as an entity. When you post a document such as this and do not want them to view other sheets, please allow Secure Sheet in Excel.

HOW TO CREATE CHARTS IN EXCEL: TYPES AND EXAMPLES?

An image is a thousand words; a chart is a thousand sets of details. Throughout this chapter, we will learn how to use the Excel graph to display our results.

What Is the Chart?

A diagram depicts details in both columns and axes. Charts are commonly used in data sets to examine trends and patterns. Let's assume that over the past three years, you have registered Excel sales figures. You can quickly see with charts which year had the largest revenue and which year had the least. You can also draw charts to compare targets with actual accomplishments.

For this chapter, we will use the following data.

Note: we're going to use Excel 2019. If you have a lower version, you may not be provided with some more advanced features.

Types of Charts

Different situations involve different forms of maps. To this end, Excel offers several chart types with which you can work. The type of chart you select depends on the type of data you want to view. To simplify things for users, Excel 2019 and above can analyze your data and make a chart type recommendation.

The table below displays some of the more popular charts and when to use them.

The Pie Chart

A Pie Chart may show just one data sequence. A sequence of data handles a row or column of charts. Excel uses the chart title (e.g., Flower) serial identification (column or row heading) and displays the values as proportional slices of the pie for that series.

When we had selected multiple data sets, Excel will disregard all but the first sets. In the next section, we have illustrated and highlighted a single data sequence in a row.

	A	B	C	D	E	F
1		1st Qtr	2nd Qtr	3rd Qtr	4th Qtr	Year
2	Flowers	$ 170	$ 240	$ 200	$ 230	$ 840
3	Shrubs	$ 220	$ 280	$ 250	$ 290	$ 1,040
4	Trees	$ 260	$ 340	$ 200	$ 320	$ 1,120

Figure 1: single series of data

The Pie Chart is distributed in subtypes. The second graph below is the 3-D pie graph, and the third is an exploded pie chart; there is also an exploded 3-D pie graph.

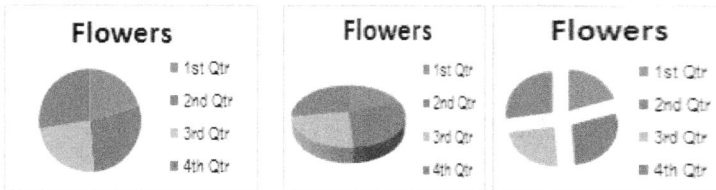

Note: it's a colored chart (although the image is black and white, you can still spot the color difference)

Some such sub-types are Pie of Pie and Bar of Pie, in which all attributes of the first pie are used to construct a second pie. To personalize the second pie's values, right-click on the section in the first pie, pick "Data Point Type," and decide how to separate the sequence.

Note that the legend of the Pie Chart includes the worksheet section headings. This may be changed by changing the headings in the worksheet or directly changing the graphic. The legend can be pushed up, down, left, center, or top right of the map ("corner" in earlier Excel versions).

The pie chart configuration may be modified to show either numerical figures or their percentages on top of the pie slices.

The Column Chart

The column map displays the contrast of one or more data points quite well. But the Clustered Column Chart is especially useful in comparing multiple data series.

We draw data points in all three series on the first graph image: Flowers, Shrubs, and Trees. As for each data set, Excel uses a specific color; we can quickly detect how a particular sequence, such as Flowers, evolves time. Yet as the columns are "clustered," the three data series may also be correlated for each time.

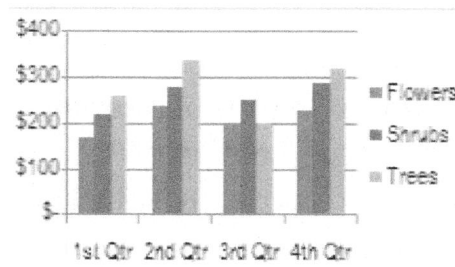

Note: it's a colored chart (although the image is black and white, you can still spot the color difference)

The vertical axis (y-axis) of a column map often indicates quantitative numbers, while the horizontal dimension (x-axis) represents time or other types. And Excel also selects the segment (the row or column headings) with the most entries on the horizontal (X-scale) scale, by example.

Nevertheless, we may pick our sort of foil — plants, shrubs, and trees — to travel along the x-axis by customizing our Excel map and the position of the four-quarters traced on the vertical axis.

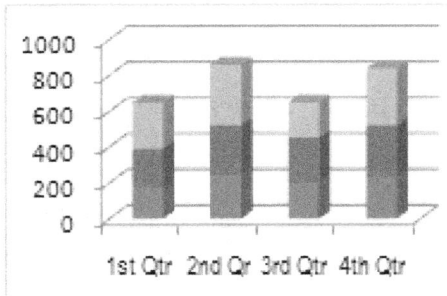

The Stacked Column Chart is one variant of this chart type. In the second picture, we display a 3-D Stacked Column Map above. In a Stacked Chart, the data points are "stacked" instead of "clustered" for each period. This type of chart shows the proportion of the total data points for every data point in the series.

The 100% Stacked Column Chart is also usable, where each value in a sequence is displayed as 100%. An illustration of a 100% Stacked Map is seen in the Bar Map segment.

Both column maps have a three-dimensional representation of the columns, as seen above in the 3-D Stacked Column Map. Another map, the "3-D Column Map," is unique since the panel itself is three dimensional, with multiple series on the X-axis, Y-axis, and Z-axis. The first illustration is a 3-D panel illustration of our data set.

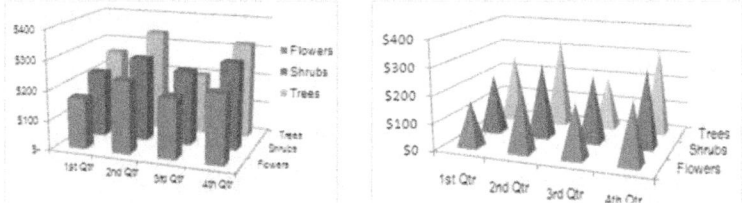

Cylinders, pyramids, and cones will be used instead of bars on most Column diagrams in older Excel models. A 3-D Pyramid Map, as seen in the second figure above.

The Line Chart

The line map displays patterns in particular. The Y-axis always displays numeric values in a line chart and time or another category in a horizontal axis (X-axis).

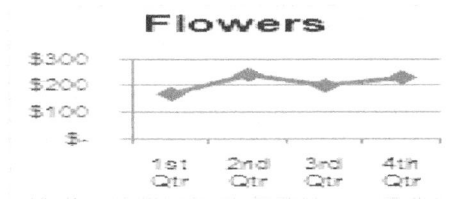

Flowers

	1st Qtr	2nd Qtr	3rd Qtr	4th Qtr
$300				
$200				
$100				
$-				

For our single series chart on the left, we selected the chart with markers. Each line chart type can be selected with or without markers. The markers are circles, squares, triangles, or other types that label the details' points. For each data series, Excel displays a unique marker — different shape and/or color.

The Line Map displays patterns for many series as successfully as seen in our map. Each line is a different color (although the image is black and white, you can still spot the color difference), as you will notice. This illustration displays a blank Line Map.

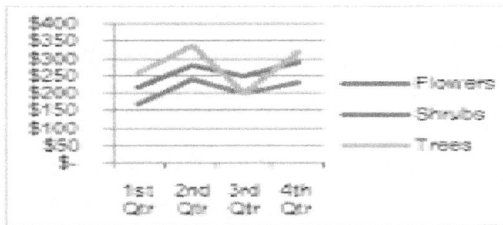

Although not as colorful as the other charts, it is easy to see how efficiently the Line Chart shows a single series trend and compares trends for multiple data values.

In addition to the Line Map, we have the Lined Line Chart with or without labels. A 3-D Line Map is available, but details in three dimensions are not seen well in the Line Chart.

The Bar Chart

The bar diagram is like a column diagram on your hand. The Bar Chart's lateral pole includes the numerical values. The first example below is the Flowers bar map for our single sequence.

When using a bar chart compared to a column chart, data and user preference depend on it. Often it's worth making all maps and contrasting the findings. Nevertheless, Bar Charts aims to display and equate a vast number of series more than certain forms of diagrams.

147

Flowers

4th Qtr

3rd Qtr

2nd Qtr

1st Qtr

$- $100 $200 $300

4th Qtr

3rd Qtr

2nd Qtr

1st Qtr

0% 50% 100%

■ Flowers
■ Shrubs
■ Trees

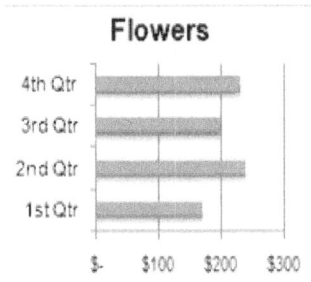

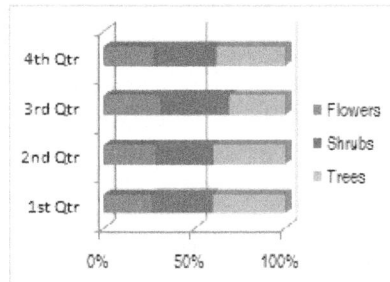

Both Bar Charts are available in 2-D and 3-D versions, but only 3-D bars are available. There is no three-dimensional bar map of three axes.

As for many forms of graphs, Excel provides the Stacked Bar Map and the Flat Column Line. The second graph above is our 100% 3D stacked bar map. Its form of the chart does not show money, but percentages on the horizontal axis. It helps one to see the percentage of every data point of 100%.

New models of Excel, along with most other chart forms, require circles, pyramids, or cones to be used instead of bars.

The Area Chart

Area maps are like line graphs so that the region underneath the map is large. Just like Line Charts, Zone Charts are primarily used to display patterns over time or certain types. The map to the left is a region map for our particular sequence.

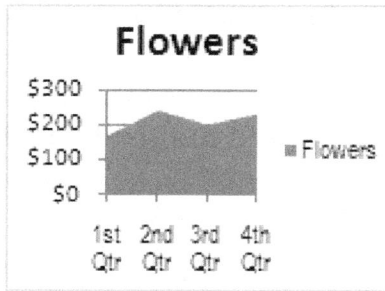

Flowers

The Area Chart, the Stacked Area Chart, and the Stacked Area Chart are three diagrams available. These charts are available in 2D format, and with the X, Y, and Z axes in true 3D format.

The following image is our 3-D field map, which displays our three series effectively.

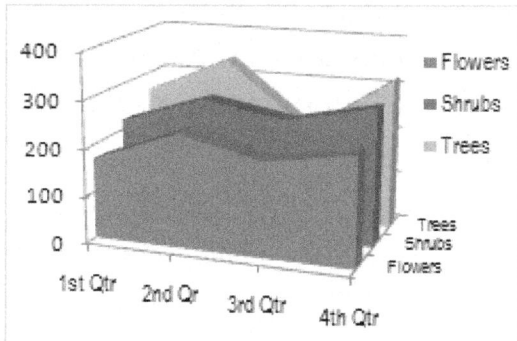

For certain instances, the Area Chart's 2-D variant does not function correctly when several sets of data are shown. Series with lower values may be concealed behind series with higher values, as seen in the first chart below. Flowers are hidden, and only a few weeks from Trees. Not a very powerful chart!

This problem is not found in the Stacked Area Chart (see below) or in the Stacked Area Chart (100%).

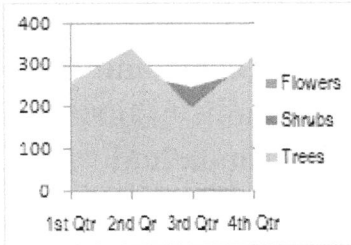

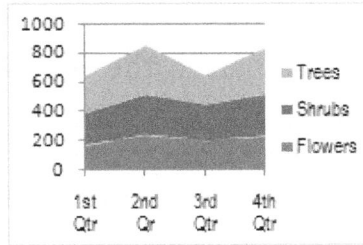

The Scatter Chart

The purpose of a dispersion chart is to examine how time or other categories the values of two series relate. To explain the scatter map, we use the following worksheet values:

	A	B	C	D	E	F	G	H	I	J	K	L	M
1		Jan	Feb	Mar	Apr	May	Jun	Jul	Aug	Sep	Oct	Nov	Dec
2	Flowers	$100	$200	$300	$500	$600	$700	$550	$475	$700	$500	$350	$400
3	Shrubs	$200	$250	$400	$600	$700	$760	$650	$550	$775	$600	$275	$200

According to Scatter Plots (U. Illinois), "Scatter plots are identical to line graphs as they use horizontal and vertical axes to display data points. However, they serve a very specific function. Scatter plots demonstrate how often each component has a different impact.

The series pair has a positive correlation if it similarly increases and a negative correlation if both decrease in the same way. They do not correlate otherwise.

Excel does not use worksheet marks to mark the horizontal axis; it only chronologically counts the X-axis.

The Scatter Chart comes in several formats: markers can indicate the data points, and the items can be connected to smooth or straight lines.

Check out our two Scatter Maps examples below. The first chart is a scattering chart with only markers; the second chart is a scattering chart with smooth lines.

In general, markers operate well when the number of data points is limited, and when the number of data points is high, straight lines without markers are sometimes used. However, it is better to seek different subtypes and see which one presents the data best.

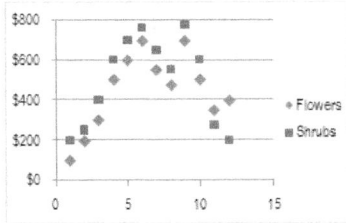

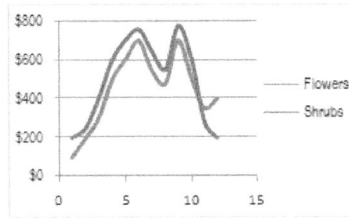

Other Chart Types

Excel offers other types of charts according to your version, but the average user doesn't use these types of charts. Some other chart types are available: Stock, Surface, Doughnut, Bubble, and Radar.

Customizing Excel Charts

Creating a regular Excel map requires a minute, but it may take a long time to modify a map if you do not obey a clear order. As Microsoft updated the Office software for the 2007 edition, the map feature was significantly enhanced. There are too many options in some ways.

The Importance of Charts

- Allows you to visualize data graphically

- Understanding trends and patterns in the charts is simpler.

- Easy to understand compared to cell results.

Step by Step Example of Creating Charts in Excel

This chapter will draw up a simple column chart showing the quantities sold against the year of sales.

- Open Excel

- Join the following sample data table.

- The workbook will look like this now.

N20	A	B	C	D	E	F
		Sales Year				
1		2012	2013	2014	2015	
2	Desktop Computers	20	12	13	12	
3	Laptops	34	45	40	39	
4	Monitors	12	10	17	15	
5	Printers	78	13	90	14	
6						
7	Items sold			Sales volumes		

You need to obey the following measures to get the required chart.

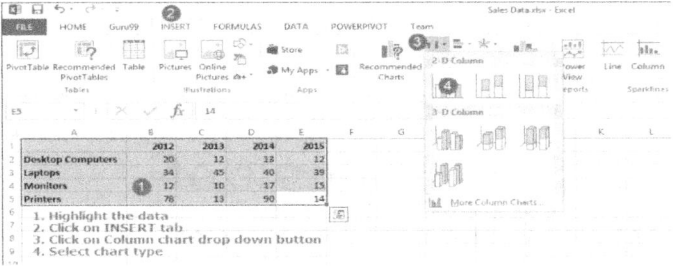

- Select the data you want to represent in a graph.

- Click on the INSERT tab from the ribbon.

- Click on the Column chart drop-down button.

- Select the chart type you want.

You should see something like this.

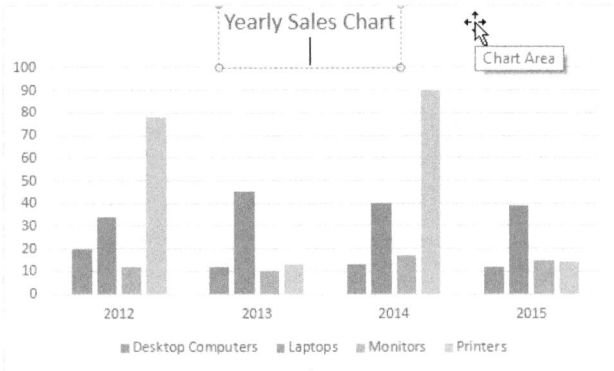

HEADERS AND FOOTERS IN A WORKSHEET

On or below the printed worksheet, you can add headers or footers in Excel. For example, you can create a footer with page numbers, date, and file name. You can create your headers or use a lot of built-in footers.

We can only spot Headers and footers in Site Design, Print Review, and typed sections. You may also use the Configuration page dialog box if the headers or footers are used with more than one worksheet at a time. You may only attach headers and footers for certain panel forms, such as schematic sheets or diagrams from the Setup Page dialog.

Add or Change Headers or Footers in Page Layout View

1. To add or change headers or footers, click on the worksheet.

2. On the Insert tab, in the Text group, click Header & Footer.

3. Tap on a left, middle, or right header or footer textbox in the top or bottom of the worksheet page to add or change a header or footer.

4. Type the new header or footer text.

Notes:

- Click Enter to start a new line in a text box header or footer.

- Use two ampersands to have a single ampersand (&) in the header or footer document. Type Subcontractors && services to have "Subcontractors and Services" in a header, for example.

- Press anywhere in the worksheet to remove headers or footers. To remove headers or footers without altering, please click on Esc.

Add or Change Headers or Footers in the Page Setup Dialog

1. To add or change headers or footers, press the worksheet or worksheets, table sheet, or map.

Tip: You can pick many worksheets by pressing Ctrl + Left. When multiple worksheets are used, the [group] appears at the top of the worksheet in the title bar.

Press every unselected worksheet to cancel a list of several worksheets in a workbook. If there is no visible unselected sheet, right-click on the selected sheet tab, and then click Ungroup Sheets.

2. On the page layout tab, click on the Launcher dialog box in the page configuration section

3. Click Custom Header or Custom Footer on the Header / Footer page.

4. To attach the header or footer details you want in this segment, click on the left, middle, or right button, and then click on either icon.

5. In the left, the middle, or right portion of the file, insert or change an additional document, or delete the current text.

Notes:

- Click Enter to start a new line in a text box header or footer.

- Use two ampersands to have a single ampersand (&) in the header or footer document. Type Subcontractors && services to have "Subcontractors and Services" in a header, for example.

FORMAT AN EXCEL TABLE

Excel provides numerous predefined table types to shape a table easily. A customized table design can be produced and added if the predefined table styles do not match your needs. Although only specific table styles should be removed, you should erase some predefined table type, and it is no longer included in a row.

The table layout choices may be further modified by choosing fast types for table components such as headers and percentages, first and last columns, banded rounds, columns, and auto filters.

Choose a Table Style

Excel can convert it to a table automatically when you pick a table type if you have a data set not formatted as a table. The configuration for an existing table can also be modified by choosing a different format.

1. Select any cell in the table or cell range to be formatted as a table.

2. Tap View as Table on the Home page.

3. Tap on the table style you would like to use.

Notes:

- Auto Preview - Excel formats the data set or table automatically with the display in every type that you choose, but only if you press Enter or you click on the mouse to validate it. You will navigate the table formats using the cursor or arrow keys on your keyboard.

- Whether you use Format as a chart, Excel transforms the data set to a chart automatically. If you do not want your data in a table to work with, you can turn it into a standard range while maintaining your table formatting.

Create or Delete a Custom Table Style

Important:

- When the design table styles are produced, the gallery Table Styles under the Design section is open.

- Different table types are not included in other workbooks but only in the existing workbook.

Create a Custom Table Style

1. Choose any cell in the table to create a personalized look.

2. On your Home page, either press Table Layout or add the Table Styles gallery from the Table Tools > Template page.

3. Click New Table Style to start the New Table Style dialog.

4. Type a name for the new table type in the Name file.

5. Take one of the following in the table item box:

- Click on the element to format an element, then click Format and select from the Font, Border, and Fill tab the formatting options you want.

- Tap on the item to delete current formatting from a document and then press on Remove.

6. In the Overview, you can see how the adjustments you made to the formatting impact the chart.

7. Select the Collection as the default table type for this document checkbox to use the existing table design as the current workbook's default table type.

Delete a Custom Table Style

1. Choose any cell in the table from which the design table type can be withdrawn.

2. On the Home page, press Format as Table, or extend the Panel Styles gallery from the Tools > Design tab.

3. Right-click on the table design you want to remove under Design, then press Delete from the shortcut list.

Note: The default table configuration includes all tables in the current workbook that use the table design.

Remove a Table Style

1. Pick any cell in the table you want to erase the current table template from.

2. Tap Layout as Table on the Home tab, or extend the Table Styles gallery from the Table Tools > Design tab (Table button on a Mac).

3. Click Clear.

The list shows up in the usual table format.

Note: Removing a table style doesn't take the table off. If you don't want to operate in a table for your details, you may transform the table to a regular range.

Choose Table Style Options to Format the Table Elements

There are many choices for table layout, which can be toggled on and off. To use one of these options:

1. Select any cell in the table.

2. Go to Table Options (tools)> Template, or Table tab on a Laptop, and check or uncheck

either of the following in the Table Type Options group:

- Header Row - Add or erase formatting in the table from the first row.

- Total Row - Quickly add a drop-down set of SUBTOTAL functions like Count, AVERAGE, List, MIN / MAX to the chart. SUBTOTAL functions require the secret rows to be used or omitted in calculations.

- First Column - Add or erase formatting in the table from the first column.

- The last Column - Add or erase formatting from the table's last column.

- Banded Rows - For fast reading, show odd and even rows of contrasting shading.

- Banded Columns - For easy reading, display odd and even columns with alternating shading.

- Filter Button - Toggle AutoFilter on and off.

HOW TO PUT A SIGNATURE ON MICROSOFT EXCEL?

Applications such as Microsoft Office provide strong tools for making and publishing records and preserving certain records. Passwords may be introduced, AutoRecovery features enabled, and signature lines inserted.

If there is a signature added to an Excel document, no edits are allowed to the document without invalidating that signature. This helps you and everyone ensure that the signer has examined and accepted a document as it is.

Adding the Signature Line

1. Tap on the signature cell you want to attach.

2. tap the "Insert" tab.

3. Select the "Signature Line" option in the "Text" section to drop-down arrow below. Tap the "Microsoft Office Signature Line" in the toolbar screen.

4. Fill in the Signature Setup box, which appears with the appropriate details. You should include the name of the signer suggested, the description of the signer suggested, the email address of the signer suggested, and any directions to the signer. You may leave any or all of these blank, but certain people reading the document can consider details about the document and the signature required vague.

5. Pick the Signature Final Settings. Next to them, you have two options with checkboxes that read "Enable the signer to attach comments in the Sign dialog box" and "Display sign date in the signature line."

The former enables the signer to type details while attaching a signature, such as a signing intent. The above incorporates the signature date into the signature envelope. Note that this is the date the document is signed, and not the date the signature box is created.

6. Click "OK" to add the signature box.

Adding the Signature

1. Open the document in Excel that needs a signature if it is not already open. Then open the

"Sign" dialog box either by double-clicking or right-clicking the signature line and choosing "sign."

2. Add signature. To do so, type in your name to add a text signature to the "X." Additionally, to navigate through a graphic edition of your written signature, click on "Pick Photo." If you are using a touch-screen tablet or other device, you can physically sign next to the "X."

3. Click "Sign" to add the signature.

Tips:

- When any signatures are omitted from the paper, they should show on the Excel window's right-hand side in a row in the "Signatures" column.

- By right-clicking on the signature line and choosing "Drop Signature," you can delete signatures. You can even erase the signature line after adding a signature.

Warning

Signers will only use a certificate authority's digital signature to sign an Office document; otherwise, someone might type in the name of the suggested signer. Microsoft's Workplace Platform provides many choices for approving certificates.

INSERT A SYMBOL

You can conveniently attach a specific character, fraction, or other icons throughout your PowerPoint slides and workbooks on Excel.

If adding icons, percentages, special characters, or foreign characters, the most crucial thing to remember is that the font you are using is essential. Not all fonts have similar characters within them. For example, while Verdana does, the Elephant font has no fractional characters in it. Consequently, it is necessary to use the right font to locate the symbol or character you like.

A Symbol such as Currency (¥), Music (♫), or Checkmarks (✔)

1. put the cursor in the file where the symbol will be inserted.

2. Go to Insert > Symbol.

3. Pick a symbol or choose More Symbols.

4. Scroll up or down to select the symbol you wish to use. Similar font sets also have various symbols, and the most frequently found symbols are in the font set for the Segoe UI. Using the Font generator above the chart of symbols to pick the font you want to search.

5. Double-click it when you select the icon you like. It integrates the icon into your register.

6. Select Close.

Tip: When you choose to render the icon bigger or smaller, pick it, and use Font Size options.

A Special Character like Em Dashes (—) or Section Marks (§)

1. Click or tap where the special character you want to insert to.

2. Go to Insert > Symbol > More Symbols.

3. Go to Special Figures.

Double-click the character you would like to insert.

Tip: Some of the different characters connected with these have shortcut keys. When you choose to use the same character in the future again, just click the shortcut key. For example, ALT+CTRL+C inserts the symbol Copyright (©).

4. Select Close.

Fractions (1/3, 2/5)

When you click them, those fractions (1/4, 1/2, and 3/4) immediately turn to a fraction character (¼, ½, ¾). Yet some don't (1/3, 2/3, 1/5, etc.), and you'll need to use the insert symbol method if you decide to use those as symbols.

1. tap where to insert the fraction.

2. Go to Insert > Symbol > More Symbols.

3. In the Subset dropdown, choose Number Forms.

Note: Not all fonts have a subset of numeric forms. When you don't see the sub-set number types usable with your font, you may need to use separate font, such as Calibri, to incorporate the character fraction.

4. Tap the fraction you want to attach double-click.

5. Select Close.

International Characters like ¿ or ü

When you also intend to type in certain languages, you might try adapting your keyboard style to that language. More information on this can be found on Allow or alter the keyboard layout language.

Within Office, there are almost all button keys for one-off characters to do so. For instance:

1. CTRL+SHIFT+ALT+? Inserts a ¿

2. CTRL+SHIFT+~ and "a" will insert ã.

3. CTRL+SHIFT+: and "u" will insert ü.

Insert a Symbol Using the Keyboard with ASCII or Unicode Character Codes

You can also use the symbol character code as a shortcut to the keyboard. Symbols and unique characters are added by using the codes ASCII or Unicode. When you look up the character code, you can see which one is.

1. Go to Insert >Symbol > More Symbols.

2. Scroll up or down the list to reach the preferred symbol; notice that you will need to adjust the font or the subset to locate it.

Tip: The font Segoe UI Symbol has a wide set of Unicode icons to select from.

3. At the right bottom, you can see character code stacks and a form. The character code is what you enter to access this icon from the keyboard, and it asks you what it is. If from: says "Unicode (hex)," the character is Unicode. If from: says "Symbol (Decimal)," then the character is ASCII.

HOW TO CHANGE PAGE SETUP?

Page configuration will make a difference when displaying your workbook in Excel; Excel offers you plenty of choices for setting up your website. The Page Layout Tab Setup group contains the following important command buttons in Excel:

- **Margins button** to pick one of three preset page margins or to configure custom margins in the Site Setup dialog box on the Margins column.

- **Guidance button** to switch between Portrait and Landscape printing mode.

- **Size button** to pick a preset paper size, set the custom scale, or adjust the print resolution or page number in the Paper Setup dialog box window.

- **Print Area button** to set and clear the print area.

- **Breaks button** to insert or remove page breaks.

- **The Background button** opens the Context dialog box that helps you pick a new graphic picture or photo to be used as a backdrop for the current worksheet. (The Remove Context button switches as soon as you choose a context image.)

- **Print Titles button** open the Sheet Tab of the Page Setup dialog box where you can identify worksheet rows to repeat at the top and worksheet columns to repeat at the left as article titles.

Changing Margins in Excel

Excel's usual margin settings for a new report include regular 3/4 inch top, bottom, left, and right margins, with slightly over 1/4 inch dividing the header and footer from the top and bottom margins, respectively.

The software allows you to select two other regular margins from the drop-down menu of the Margins icon beside the Standard margin settings:

Broad margins of 1 inch top, bottom, left and right margins, and 1/2 inch dividing header and footer respectively from the top and bottom margins.

Narrow margins with 3/4 "top and bottom margins and 1/4" left and right margins with 0.3 "separating header and foot from the top and bottom margins, respectively.

You often come across a report that takes up a full printed page, and then just enough to spill over to a second, mostly empty, page. To push the last column or the last few rows of the worksheet details into Page 1, attempt to pick Narrow from the drop-down menu in Excel on the Margins tab.

If that does not work, you should try changing the margins for posting from the Page Setup dialog box's Margins tab manually or moving the margin markers in the Print screen display region in the Backstage view (Press Ctrl + P and press the Display Margins button). Attempt to lower left and right margins to get more columns on a list. Try raising the top and bottom margins to get more rows on a list.

To access the Page Setup dialog box Margins tab in Excel 2019, pick Custom Margins from the drop-down menu on the Margins icon. In the text boxes Top, Middle, Left, and Right, join the previous settings — or pick the existing margin settings with their spinner buttons, respectively.

WHAT ARE THE "BRING ELEMENTS FORWARD" AND "BRING ELEMENTS BACK" OPTIONS?

Once you add photographs, forms, or other objects to your Office papers, they stack in separate layers automatically when you add them. You may transfer the individual shapes or other items or entity classes in a row.

For instance, within a stack, you can push items up or down one layer at a time, or transfer them in one step to the top or bottom of a stack. When you draw items, you will combine them to produce various results.

Notes:

- See Align or arrange an image, shape, text box, or WordArt for specific object alignment.

- For grouping detail, see Group or ungroup forms, pictures, or other artifacts.

Move a Picture, Shape, Text Box, or WordArt

- Select the WordArt border, text box, or form you want to pass. To push several textboxes or forms, when clicking on boundaries, press and hold Ctrl.

- Move it to a different position as the mouse moves to the four-headed button.

Click and hold Ctrl when holding an arrow key, to push in tiny increments. Then just push then hold Shift as you drag it, to shift the target horizontally or vertically.

Note: The incremental, or nudge, distance is an increase of 1 pixel. The percentage of the zoom depends on what 1 screen pixel represents relative to the document region.

When zooming your document to 400 percent, 1 screen pixel on the document is a relatively small nudge distance. When zooming your document to 25 percent, 1 screen pixel on the document is a relatively large nudge distance.

This may be quicker to cut and paste this, based on how fast you push the WordArt, form, or text box. Right-click on the link, then press Cut (or Ctrl+X). Click Ctrl+V to print. You may also cut and paste it into a separate paper or within programs, such as an Excel worksheet from a PowerPoint slide.

Move a Text Box, WordArt, or Shape Forward or Backward in a Stack

- Click the WordArt, form, or text box you'd like to push up or down the row.

- Click on either Put Forward or Submit Backward in the Type Drawing Resources window.

- You can push the object up to one layer (Bring Forward) or up from the stack (Bring Front). Backward has similar sending options: one layer down (Send Backward) or one layer down to the bottom of the pile (Send Back).

Tips:

In-Office 2016 and Office 2019, it may be easier to use up and down arrows in the Selection Pane to move objects if you have a lot of WordArt, shapes, text boxes, or other objects.

The search panel is not accessible in Office 2010 or Project.

SORTING, GROUPING, AND FILTERING CELLS

A spreadsheet with Microsoft Excel will provide a lot of details. Often you can notice that to be able to use it more efficiently. You need to reorder or organize the information, build classes, or filter the information.

Sorting

Sorting lists is a simple activity in the spreadsheet, helping you to reorder your info quickly. The most popular sorting method is alphabetic ordering, which can be performed in ascending or descending order.

To Sort in Alphabetical Order

- choose a cell in the column you need to sort (We select a cell in column A in this example).

- On the Home tab, click the Sort & Filter command in the Edit Section.

- Click Sort A to Z. Now, the knowledge is ordered in alphabetic order in the Group section.

To Sort from Smallest to Largest

- Select a cell in the column you want to sort (a column with numbers).

- On the Home tab, click the Sort & Filter command in the Edit Section.

- Select Limit to Major. Now the knowledge is arranged from the smallest number to the largest.

- Through selecting From Largest to Smallest in the chart, you will select in reverse numerical order.

To Sort Multiple Levels

- Click the Sort & Filter command in the Home Tab Editing Unit.

- Pick Custom Sort from the dialog box to open the chart.

OR

- Select the Data Tab.

- Locate the Sort and Filter group.

- To open the Custom Sort dialog, tap the Order command. You can filter them by one object or multiple items from here.

- Tap the drop-down arrow in the Column Sort by field, then select one of the options—in this example, Category.

- Choose what you want to focus on. We'll leave the default as Value in this case.

- Choose how the tests should be organized. Leave it as A to Z, so alphabetically it is ordered.

- Tap Add Level to add another element.

- Select a column choice Then by region. We have chosen Unit Cost in this case.

- Choose what to type. We will leave the default as Value in this case.

- Select how to order the results. Leave it as smallest to largest.

- Tap OK.

They arranged the file. Both divisions are grouped in alphabetical order, and the unit expense is listed from the smallest to the largest within each division.

Bear in mind that all the knowledge and documentation is always here — it's only in another sequence.

Grouping Cells Using the Subtotal Command

Grouping is a useful feature of Excel, which gives you control over how the information is displayed. You have to figure them out before you can meet. In this segment, we'll learn how to use the Subtotal command to build classes.

- To create groups with subtotals:

- Select any cell with information in it.

- Tap on the Data tab to Subtotal order. The details are correctly picked in the database, and the subtotal dialog box appears.

- Decide if you like things to come together. We will organize this by Category in this case.

- Select a function. We will leave the SUM function selected.

- Pick the section you like to see the Subtotal in. In this case, you select Total Cost by default.

- Tap OK. The chosen cells are packed into groups with subtotals.

To Collapse or Display the Group

- Tap the black minus sign, which is the hide detail icon, to collapse the group.

- Tap the black plus sign, which is the show detail icon, to expand the group.

- To collapse and view the community, use the Show Information and Hidden Information command in the Outline category.

To Ungroup Select Cells

- Choose the cells you want to remove from the group.

- Tap the Ungroup command.

- Choose Ungroup from the list. A dialog box will appear.

- Tap OK.

- To ungroup the entire worksheet:

- Choose all cells with grouping.

- Tap Clear Outline from the menu.

- Filtering cells.

- Data in a spreadsheet is simple to filter or temporarily hide. This lets you focus on different table entries.

Filtering Data

- On the Data window, press the order button. Drop-down arrows appear next to any heading in the panel.

- Click the drop-down arrow next to your desired filter heading. For example, if you only want to see the Flavors info, click the drop-down arrow next to Category.

- Uncheck Select All.

- Choose Flavor.

- Tap OK. All other data will be filtered, obscured, or available only to Flavor data.

- One filter clear:

- Pick one of the arrows next to the filtered column.

- Choose Clear Filter.

Note: To remove all filters, click the Filter command.

Filtering may look like grouping, but the difference is that if you want to, you can now filter onto another field. Let's assume you only want to see the vanilla-related colors, for starters.

Just click the arrow next to Item, then select Text Filters. Take Contains from the menu if you want to include every entry that includes the term vanilla. A dialog box pops up. Choose coconut, then OK. Now we can see that the data is filtered again and that only the flavors related to vanilla appear.

PROTECT A WORKSHEET

You should encrypt the cells on the Excel worksheet and then secure the sheet with a password to deter certain users from inadvertently or intentionally modifying, transferring, or removing data inside a worksheet. Perhaps you own the worksheet for the project progress survey, where you want team leaders to apply details just to particular cells and not be allowed to change anything else. With worksheet security, you can modify only some document sections, and users cannot change data in any other area on the document.

Important

- Protection at the worksheet level is not meant as a safety feature. This also prevents users from changing locked cells within the worksheet.

- Securing a worksheet is not the same as securing a password-laden Excel file or a workbook. For further details, please see below:

- See Encrypt an Excel file to lock the file so that other users can not access it.

- See Protecting a Workbook to prevent users from inserting, changing, transferring, copying, or hiding / unhiding sheets inside a workbook.

- See Privacy and Security in Excel to know the difference in securing the Excel script, workbook, or worksheet.

Choose what Cell Elements You Want to Lock

Here's everything you should put into an unprotected sheet:

- **Formulas:** If you don't want to see your formulas from other users, you can hide them from being seen in the cells or the Formula bar. For more details, see Display or hide formulas.

- **Ranges:** Inside a safe sheet, you can encourage users to operate under different ranges. See Unlock or activate different places inside a safe worksheet for more detail.

Note: When you connect them to a list, ActiveX monitors, type monitors, forms, maps, SmartArt, Sparklines, Slicers, Timelines, to name a couple, are already mounted. But the lock will only work if you allow for sheet protection. For more details about how to allow sheet security, please see the following link.

Enable Worksheet Protection

Worksheet protection is a two-step process: first, unlock cells that others can edit, and then, with or without a password, you can protect the worksheet.

Step 1: Unlock any Cells that Need to Be Editable

1. Select the worksheet tab you want to cover in your Excel file.

2. Choose the cells that others can edit.

Tip: You can choose multiple, non-contiguous cells by pressing Ctrl + Left-Click.

3. Right-click somewhere on the sheet and pick Layout Cells (or using Ctrl+1 or Command+1 on the Mac), then move to the Locked Security page.

Step 2: Protect the Worksheet

Next, pick the behavior that users can take on the document, such as adding or removing columns or lists, modifying items, sorting, or using AutoFilter, to list a couple.

You may also assign a password that will encrypt the worksheet. A password stops anyone from withdrawing security from the worksheet — it has to be inserted to unprotect the document.

The steps to protect your sheet are provided below.

1. On the Review tab, click Protect Sheet.

2. Pick the elements you want people to be able to alter from in the Enable all users of this worksheet to display.

Option Allows Users to

Select locked cells: Moving the pointer to cells in the protection column of the prototype cells dialog. The users can pick the locked cells by design.

Select unlocked cells: Shift the pointer to cells for which the Locked box is unchecked on the Format Cells dialog box's Protection Tab. Users can choose unlocked cells by default, and they can press the TAB key to move between unlocked cells on a protected worksheet.

Format cells: Change any of the Format Cells options or the Conditional Formatting dialog boxes. If you applied conditional formatting before protecting the worksheet, the formatting would continue to change when a user enters a value that satisfies another condition.

Format columns: Using all of the commands for column layout, like adjusting column width or covering columns (home row, party cells, button Format).

Format rows: Using some of the commands for formatting the table, like adjusting row height or hiding rows (home page, community cells, Button format).

Columns insert: Insert columns.

Attach lines: Add lines.

Insert hyperlinks: Insert new hyperlinks also in cells that have been activated.

Columns Delete: Delete columns.

Note: If Remove columns are protected and Insert columns are not protected, then a user can insert columns, but they cannot be deleted.

Delete rows: Delete rows.

Note: If Remove rows are protected and Insert rows are not protected, then a user can insert rows, but they cannot be deleted.

Sort: Use some data sorting commands (Data tab, Sort & Filter group).

Note: No matter this environment, users cannot sort ranges that contain locked cells on a safe worksheet.

Use AutoFilter: When using AutoFilters, using the drop-down arrows to adjust the filter on ranges.

Note: No matter this environment, users can't add or delete AutoFilter on a safe worksheet.

Use PivotTable reports: Format, switch the layout, refresh or otherwise modify reports on PivotTable, or create new reports.

Edit objects; Doing any of the following:

- Make changes to graphic objects that you did not unlock before you protected the worksheet, including maps, embedded charts, shapes, text boxes, and controls. For example, if a worksheet has a button running a macro, you can click the button to execute the macro, but you can't delete it.

- Allow some improvements to an embedded map, such as the layout. The map will continue to be changed when you adjust the data from the source.

- Add or edit notes.

Sample of an Edit scene: Look at possibilities you've covered, make adjustments to possibilities you've avoided improvements to, and erase certain scenarios. If the cells are not secured, users may adjust the evolving cells' values and introduce new scenarios.

3. Optionally type a password to unprotect the sheet box in the File and press OK. In the Confirm Password dialog box, enter the password and click OK.

Important

- Using good passwords mixing upper case letters, numbers, and icons with lower case letters. Weak passwords do not mix those elements. Passwords will have spans of 8 characters or longer. A passphrase that uses 14 characters or more would be better.

- Bearing in mind your password is important. If you forget your password, Microsoft will not be able to retrieve it.

BASIC MATH IN EXCEL: ADDITION, SUBTRACTION, MULTIPLICATION, AND DIVISION

Are you new to Excel and don't know where the formulas and operations are going to begin? Many tablets use simple maths: add and deduct figures, or calculate and division. Understanding these mathematical formulas will help you to manipulate your Excel data by graduating to more complex equations.

How Does Basic Math Work in Excel?

Excel uses formulas to control info or functions. A feature must enter the cell's contents plus some operating symbols to tell the data what to do. A single cell can be input into a multi-cell feature or set.

The Total method may be used for extra, subtraction, multiplication, and division. Your input is a simple mathematical term for the calculation Number. Here is a sample from this:

=SUM (A1-A2)

This feature, translated into understandable English, means: "Calculate the amount of the number in cell A1 less the number in cell A2."

Basic math doesn't actually require working with the SUM function. In certain instances, you can miss the format "= SUM)" (and simply type "= A1+A2" in the function code. However, if you are new to formulas, you also have to use the SUM function and good practice.

Adding Numbers

To add SUM numbers, use the plus (+) symbol.

=SUM (A1+A2)

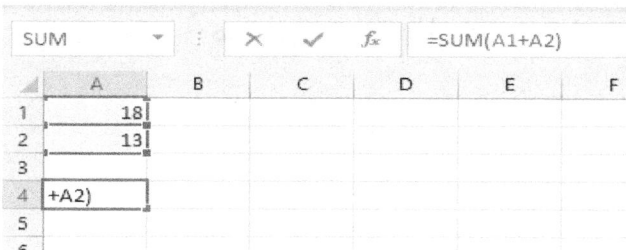

Know you are not confined to adding only two numbers. You can add many numbers together and chain them along with plus signs, and you can add a whole range of adjacent cells together with a colon (:). For instance:

=SUM (E1: E4)

✕	✓	*fx*	=SUM(E1:E4)	

C	D	E	F
	June	$ 500.00	
	July	$ 800.00	
	August	$ 200.00	
	September	$ 500.00	
	Total:	E4)	

This formula says, "Calculate the number of E1 to E4 cells."

Subtracting Numbers

Subtraction functions the same as inserting, except that you use the sign minus-).

=SUM (A1-A2)

A4		:	✕	✓	fx	=SUM(A1-A2)	

	A	B	C	D	E	F
1	18					
2	13					
3						
4	A2)					
5						
6						

And you can mix subtraction with an addition like this:

=SUM (A1-A2+A3)

SUM		:	✕	✓	fx	=SUM(A1-A2+A3)	

	A	B	C	D	E	F
1	18					
2	13					
3	5					
4						
5	A2+A3)					
6						
7						

Multiplying Numbers

To multiply, using an asterisk (*) as the operator for multiplication. In the example below, we multiplied the total number of hours by an hourly rate to get a final total. Note here that "Complete hours" are many cells E1 through E4 in cell E5 itself.

=SUM (E5*E6)

			fx	=SUM(E5*E6)	
	C	D		E	F
		June		10.00	
		July		5.00	
		August		13.00	
		September		8.00	
		Total Hrs		36.00	
		Rate/hr	$	50.00	
		Total:	E6)		

Dividing Numbers

Division once again works the same multiplication except that you use a forward slash (/) as the division operator.

=SUM (E7/2)

			fx	=SUM(E7/2)	
	C	D		E	F
		June		10.00	
		July		5.00	
		August		13.00	
		September		8.00	
		Total Hrs		36.00	
		Rate/hr	$	50.00	
		Total:		$1,800.00	
		Downpayment:	2)		

Complex Equations

If you want to chain addition and subtraction together in a single equation with multiplication and division, you will need to use parentheses to denote which operations are done first. The operations in parentheses are done first — so if you have several nested parentheses, the longest parentheses are conducted first, then the approximation makes its way "outward."

For example, claim you want the number of cells E1 to E4 multiplied by the number of cells F1 to F3. You want to add up first the two sums you are multiplying, and then multiply.

=SUM ((E1:E4)*(F1:F3))

We use the cell ranges here (e.g., "E1: E4") as a shorthand for addition. The SUM function will add that range of cells automatically. Here is an example where subtraction is used before multiplication:

=SUM ((A1-A2)*(F1:F3))

And here, we deduct A2 from A3 and then calculate the consequence by the number of cells F1 to F3.

Are you ever confused? The basic things to remember are that you are doing cell content operations. You apply to the cells and instead use a math operator (+, -, * or /) to signify what to do with the numbers in certain cells. Using the Total feature is fine because, for the easiest situations, you should miss it and type in math formulas on your own.

Calculate the Percentage of a Total

Suppose the company has quarterly revenue of 125,000 euros and you want to ask what proportion of the amount is 20,000 euros.

1. that is what you measure by dividing 20,000 by 125,000. In cell C2, you can see the formula: = B2/ A2. The result is shown as 0.16 because a percentage of cell C2 is not formatted.

	A	B	C
1	Totaal verkoop	Welk percentage van het totaal is € 20.000?	
2	€ 125.000,00	€ 20.000,00	0,16

2. To format as 0.16 percent, also delete the none, press the Percentage Start key.

If you use Excel for the web, please click Start Excel for the Numbering > percentage.

So you will see that €20,000 is €125,000 at 16 percent.

	A	B	C
1	Totaal verkoop	Welk percentage van het totaal is € 20.000?	
2	€ 125.000,00	€ 20.000,00	16%

Tip: Notation is the crux of percentage-showing answers. See Numbers as percentages for more information.

Calculate the Difference Percentage Between Two Numbers

In 2011, one company had sales of €485,000 and in 2012 of €598,634. What is the difference in percentage between these two years?

1. Click first to add the percent notation to the cell in cell B3. Select Start Percentage click on the column.

If you use Excel for the web, please click Start Excel for the Numbering > percentage.

	A	B
1	Verkoop 2011	Verkoop 2012
2	€ 485.000,00	€ 598.634,00
3		23%

2. In cell B3, divide second-year turnover (€598,634.00) by first-year turnover (€485,000.00) and subtract 1 from that.

3. In cell C3, this is the solution. = (B2/2002) -1. The percentage gap is 23 percent between the two figures.

Note the B2 / A2 braces. First, it determines what is in brackets, and then 1 is subtracted.

HOW TO INSERT CURRENCY SYMBOLS IN EXCEL?

You can Simple use Insert > Symbol to add several different kinds of symbols.

Step 1

Make sure the Excel recognizes certain cells as currencies once you have inputted the numbers. Select your cells, and select Currency from the dropdown menu on the Number section in the Home tab.

Step 2

All the numbers are now branded with the default currency — dollars in my case. Choose the cells which include the currency you want to change. Right-click on the cells and then click Format.

Step 3

On the Number tab, a popup window should appear, and Currency should already be picked. Choose your currency from the dropdown menu for Icons. (You can even adjust the two decimal places norm if you really want to.)

You will also be able to display multiple currency symbols on the same Excel sheet.

How to Change the Currency Symbol for Certain Cells in Excel?

If you function with one Excel file for various currencies, you'll need to adjust the currency icon on certain columns, without impacting certain columns. You can conveniently use several currency symbols for formatting "Currency" in the same Excel table board.

Note: If you use the same currency symbol throughout your Excel spreadsheets, you can change the default currency symbol over Windows. This is for circumstances when you want two separate currency symbols in the same file.

- Make sure that the numbers involved are formatted as currency before doing anything else. To do so, pick the cells that you want to format.

- Then, in the "Number" section of the "Home" tab, select "Currency" from the "Number Format" drop-down list.

- The numbers in the cells selected are all formatted as currency with the default currency symbol applied by Windows.

- To change certain currency numbers to another currency type, such as Euros, select the cells that you want to change.

- Click the "Number Type" button in the lower-right corner of the screen in the "Item" column of the "Home" page.

- "Currency" should be selected on the "Number" tab in the "Class" column. Click the drop-down list of "Symbol," scroll down to the "Euro" options and choose one if you want the Euro symbol before or after the number depends. Click the "OK" button.

- A different currency symbol is added to the chosen amounts.

- You may have noticed a drop-down list that has a currency symbol on it in the "Number" section of the "Home" tab. This can appear like a simpler way for the chosen cells to adjust the currency symbol. But this is the "Accounting Number Format," not the default currency format.

- If you select "Euro" from the drop-down list of "Accounting Number Format," you will get Euro symbols on your numbers, but they will show up in the accounting format that aligns the decimal points in a column. Notice that the currency symbols next to the numbers are not correct. They are left-aligned, instead.

- In the "Number" tab in the "Format Cells" dialog box, you can also adjust the number of decimal places and the size of negative numbers.

HOW TO ACTIVATE THE THOUSANDS SEPARATOR IN EXCEL?

1. Choose the cells that you are trying to format.

2. On the Home tab, tap the Dialog Box next to Number.

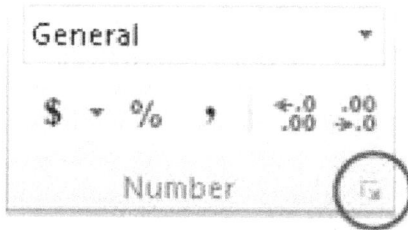

3. check the Number tab, in the Category list, click Number.

4. To view or hide the various separator, choose or clear the Use 1000 Separator (,) and check the box.

Tip: To display the thousands of separators quickly, On the Home tab in the group number, you can tap the Comma Style picture button.

Note: By default, Excel uses the thousands of commas as the system separator. You can, however, specify a different system separator in Excel.

HOW TO CREATE A SCHEDULE IN EXCEL?

Microsoft Excel may offer what appear to be tasks for a single user – creating spreadsheets, designing invoices, running calculations.

Yet Excel can be a perfect way to communicate with others on project schedules, keep track of where essential company operations are at some moment, and create strategic planning.

Excel gets you going by providing a range of models that you can tailor to fit the project's needs, meaning you won't need to start from scratch. See how Microsoft Excel makes up the designs.

1.

Open Microsoft Excel, click on the "Zip" tab and pick "New." On the Accessible Templates, screen click on the "Schedules" icon.

2.

Double-click either the file folder "Business Plans" or "Timelines" and search the Excel templates open. Choose one that suits your business best, but bear in mind that you can fully customize the text, event placement, and other parts of the project. It opens in the Excel file window after you double-click the Plan template.

3.

Check for any wrong template elements you don't need for your projects, such as note boxes, graphics, or portions of a timeline. Click on each and press to remove the "Delete" key.

4.

Click on the schedule in the first box or area and type the project's first part, or where you are currently in the project process, such as "Kickoff Meeting."

5.

Move to the next section of the timetable and type the next step or task. This is also where you can type the name of the employee associated with that part of the project and any notes, such as "80 percent complete" or "8/1/2012 Customer called."

6.

Continue filling in the project's main points to the predicted endpoint. If required, display the project points are full by clicking on the timeline of the project cell or box and then clicking on the "Fill Color" button on the ribbon of the "Back" page.

The icon, which looks like a can of tipping paint, offers various colored squares. Click on one of the squares to indicate certain times in your schedule, such as green for completed project parts, and red for overdue or late projects.

7.

Check on the template for a placeholder title. In those cells, highlight and replace your text, including date and the project manager's name, if you wish.

8.

Click on the "File" tab and select "Save As." Naming the file with a date may also be helpful, so you know it is the project starting point. Click on the 'Save' button.

Throughout the project, you can reopen the file, mark some items late or complete, add parts to the project, and reserve the file with a new date. This offers you an immediate at-a-glance, versioned glimpse at all phases of the project.

Tip: When other employees are involved in your project, you might also want to make your Excel project scheduler available to them. This can be as easy as storing the file in the company intranet, but keep in mind that this ensures that workers can access it and make adjustments.

If you want to limit entry, you might want to set up a specific day of the week when workers send your updates to the department. Change the timetable for the Excel project, if necessary.

HOW TO ADD A COLUMN OR ROW IN EXCEL?

Insert or Delete a Column

1. Select any cell in the list, go to Home > Insert > Insert Columns or Delete Sheets of columns.

2. Optionally, right-click the column top and select Insert or Remove.

Insert or Delete a Row

1. choose any cell within the row, then go to Home > Insert > Insert Sheet Rows or Delete Sheet Rows.

2. optional, right-click the row number, and then choose Insert or Delete.

Formatting Options

While you pick a formatting row or column, that formatting is transferred to a new row or column that you are inserting. If you do not want the formatting to be added, after entering, you may

click the Insert Options button and pick one of the
following choices:

	A	B	C	D	E
1	Data1		Data2	Data3	Data
2	0.01871		9551	0.323264	0.21415
3	0.187181		◉ Format Same As Left		5
4	0.86551		○ Format Same As Right		8
5	0.79091				9
6	0.278499		○ Clear Formatting		1

If the Insert Options button is not visible, go to
File > Options > Advanced > in the Cut, Copy and
Paste group, then check the option Show Insert
Options.

HOW TO COUNT THE NUMBER OF TIMES A WORD APPEARS IN EXCEL?

Excel formulas and functions allow you to expand the framework by applying your own, personalized operations to the results. You may use them inside a spreadsheet or in an external spreadsheet to conduct calculations on individual cells. You can also use them in Excel to count duplicate values, such as the number of times a word appears in a group of cells or a whole spreadsheet.

Excel Formulas and Functions

An Excel formula is an expression inserted into a cell by first clicking "=." An equivalent symbol accompanies an expression acting on the values of another cell or set of cells. An Excel feature is an embedded formula that executes a specific task. Microsoft provides a variety of functions that make the development of spreadsheets simpler for consumers.

An example of a definition is "=A1+A2+A3+A4," which integrates values in A1 to A4 cells. This is a perfectly valid formula, but by using the SUM function, which adds the values of two cells or a list of cells, you could shorten it. By entering "= SUM (A1: A4)," you obtain the same addition as "= A1+A2+A3+A4" using the SUM function.

Use Countif in Excel to Count Frequency of Values

In Excel, the Countif function returns the number of times within a range of cells a certain condition is met. One of the common conditions is to match the cell's value to a particular value, which is how it can be used to count the frequency a value occurs. The value can be either a number or a string. Note that when comparing strings, COUNTIF ignores the upper and lower cases. This means being counted as matching "apples" and "APPLES."

When you use the function COUNTIF to match a value, you type in a range of cells and the value. For example, if the word Seattle is found, "= COUNTIF (A1: A4," Seattle)" "will check cells A1 through A4 and increment a counter. When the function is finished, it returns the counter value.

The COUNTIF function can be used to create longer and more complex formulas such as "= COUNTIF (A2: A5," bananas) "+ COUNTIF (A2: A5," oranges)," "which adds the number of times that the word "bananas" is found to the number of times that the word "oranges" appears.

Counting Word Frequency in Rows and Columns

Without defining a limit, you can use the called limit function in Excel as to the number of occurrences in a column or section. Choose a column by clicking the letter at the top of the whole row by clicking on the number on the left. Click on the Formulas tab on the Define Name button, and enter a name in the New Name dialog. This name can then be used to refer to all of the cells in the row or column.

Say you use Define Name, for example, to add the name "NamesCol" to a column. By entering "= COUNTIF (NamesCol, "Mary"), you can count all the times the name "Mary" occurs in the cells in the column using the defined name. Each time you add a new value to a cell in the NamesCol column, the result of the formula will be updated automatically.

Counting Characters in a Cell

There are other drawbacks to the COUNTIF feature: you cannot use it to count individual characters. The role can scan inside a cell for strings but not for characters in a cell set. Then use the roles LEN and SUBSTITUTE. The formula for searching for all occurrences of the letter "a" in cell A1 is "= LEN (A1) − LEN (SUBSTITUTE (A1," a, "). "If cell A1 contains the string" banana, "the formula returns 3.

This formula works by using the LEN function to take the string length within the cell. Then SUBSTITUTE is used to remove all of the "a" characters from the string. The current string's duration is subtracted from the previous one. The consequence is the amount of character "a" occurrences.

FREEZE PANES TO LOCK ROWS AND COLUMNS

To hold a worksheet section, open when navigating to another region of the worksheet, go to the View tab, where you can Freeze Panes to lock different rows and columns in place or Split panes to build separate windows on the same worksheet.

Freeze rows or columns

Freeze the First Column

- Select View > Freeze Panes > Freeze First Column.

The blurred line between Column A and B shows that the first column is being frozen.

Freeze the First Two Columns

- Select the third column.

- Select View > Freeze Panes > Freeze Panes.

Freeze Columns and Rows

- Pick the cell below the circles and the columns that you want to hold clear while moving to the right.

- Select View > Freeze Panes > Freeze Panes.

Unfreeze Rows or Columns

On the View tab > Window > Unfreeze Panes.

Note: Excel Starter would probably be used if you don't see the View tab. In Excel Starter, not all functions are supported.

CONVERT A TEXT FILE OR CSV FILE INTO AN EXCEL SPREADSHEET

Using Microsoft Excel to save the contact details saved in a delimited TXT or CSV file in an Excel tab to render editing simpler

Constant Contact fully supports uploading to an Excel spreadsheet (XLS or XLSX), a text file (TXT), or a comma-separated value file (CSV), but there may be times when you want to convert a TXT or CSV file of contact information first. Using an Excel spreadsheet allows reading and interacting with your data much simpler if you need to make changes before importing them, particularly if your contact list is on the larger side.

Differences Between TXT, CSV, and XLS File Types

Based on the use, text files, CSV files, and Excel spreadsheets are perfect ways to store data:

- Text File (TXT) - Data files contain plain text and are commonly created with either NotePad (PC) or TextEdit (Mac). When you insert material into a text file, it can strip both types and formatting, leaving you only plain text. This allows copying and pasting data fast without issues with the layout. If you paste data from the spreadsheet into a TXT file, it will be separated by tabbed spaces.

- Comma Separated Value File (CSV) - A CSV file also includes plain text and is portable, since it can be accessed on any operating device, in any text editor, and spreadsheet programs like Excel as well. If you paste data from the spreadsheet into a CSV file, it is separated by commas.

- Excel Spreadsheet (XLS) —Excel spreadsheet apps, such as Google Sheets or OpenOfficeCalc, can only open Excel spreadsheets, but they have loads of formatting choices, ways to measure data by functions, and ways to display data visually by charts and tables. Information collected in a spreadsheet is split into cells, rows, and columns.

Steps to Convert Content from a TXT or CSV File into Excel

The process for importing a TXT or CSV file into Excel is identical for Excel 2007, 2010, 2013, 2016, and 2019:

- Open the Excel table to save data and press the Data button.

- In the Get External Data group, tap From Text.

- Pick the TXT or CSV file you want to convert and tap Import.

- Pick "Delimited." A limit is just an excellent way of saying that your TXT file uses tabs or that your CSV file uses commas to separate and group your details.

- Tap Next.

- Pick the delimiter that groups your data into individual columns in the Data preview field. Typically, you want to pick "Tab" when converting a TXT file and "Comma" when converting a CSV file.

Note: If you pick "Space," When the text column header has several words, it will often split a single column into several columns.

For instance, the column "First Name" becomes a column "First" and a column "Name." See the Data Review carefully to ensure that the data is compatible with the column header!

- Tap Next.

- Pick "General."

- Tap Finish.

- Choose "Existing Worksheet."

- Add "=A1" to the field. It means that the data begins in row 1, column A of the table. If there are blank rows on the table above your results, a file import error will occur.

- Tap OK.

- Tap Save.

ADVANCED FORMATTING TRICKS FOR EXCEL USERS

When you know some advanced coding techniques, your worksheets will be more polished and easier to read.

Most consumers of Excel know-how to implement simple numerical and text formats. Yet users move beyond the basics would increase the readability and productivity of sheets. Understanding how to add exactly the correct formatting rapidly and conveniently to individual cells also allows users to function more effectively. Those five tips should enable users to learn more from the design features of Excel.

1: Use the Fill Handle to Copy Formatting

The fill handle is a strong and flexible instrument. With only a few quick clicks, the fill handle can copy formats, in addition to copying formulas and creating series:

- Pick the cell you want to copy and contains the formatting. I selected A2 in Figure A to copy the bold font and the grey fill color to the remaining cells in column A.

- Double-click the handle that fills the cell. By overwriting the TOTALS code with January, the fill handle's sequence action has clicked into gear. Don't worry; you can undo this next one.

- Click the corresponding AutoFill Options Control to view the list shown in Figure B.

- Choose the Fill Formatting Only option.

Figure A

	A	B	C	D	E	F
		Smith	Jones	Michaels	Hancock	Totals
1						
2	January	$4,212.64	$6,795.69	$2,148.78	$4,611.14	$17,768.25
3	February	$3,194.08	$3,449.36	$9,020.05	$7,401.84	$23,065.33
4	March	$3,000.00	$2,332.71	$8,507.84	$4,224.17	$18,064.72
5	April	$2,500.00	$2,804.82	$9,078.84	$7,620.23	$22,003.89
6	May	$2,989.75	$2,504.17	$4,263.65	$2,706.73	$12,464.30
7	June	$3,200.34	$5,426.36	$5,325.03	$4,494.94	$18,446.68
8	July	$6,912.61	$4,229.14	$6,361.90	$5,936.46	$23,440.11
9	August	$4,596.56	$5,936.79	$3,222.88	$3,304.52	$17,060.75
10	September	$7,529.99	$7,673.70	$2,862.51	$3,831.45	$21,897.65
11	October	$5,188.08	$9,840.23	$2,489.00	$6,686.40	$24,203.70
12	November	$3,085.00	$2,209.72	$5,197.35	$3,495.50	$13,987.57
13	December	$3,656.00	$4,578.77	$938.35	$7,961.63	$17,134.76
14	TOTALS	$50,065.06	$57,781.45	$59,416.19	$62,275.01	$229,537.71

Figure B

	A	B	C	D	E	F	G
1		Smith	Jones	Michaels	Hancock	Totals	
2	January	$4,212.64	$6,795.69	$2,148.78	$4,611.14	$17,768.25	
3	February	$3,194.08	$3,449.36	$9,020.05	$7,401.84	$23,065.33	
4	March	$3,000.00	$2,332.71	$8,507.84	$4,224.17	$18,064.72	
5	April	$2,500.00	$2,804.82	$9,078.84	$7,620.23	$22,003.89	
6	May	$2,989.75	$2,504.17	$4,263.65	$2,706.73	$12,464.30	
7	June	$3,200.34	$5,426.36	$5,325.03	$4,494.94	$18,446.68	
8	July	$6,912.61	$4,229.14	$6,361.90	$5,936.46	$23,440.11	
9	August	$4,596.56	$5,936.79	$3,222.88	$3,304.52	$17,060.75	
10	September	$7,529.99	$7,673.70	$2,862.51	$3,831.45	$21,897.65	
11	October	Copy Cells	840.23	$2,489.00	$6,686.40	$24,203.70	
12	November	Fill Series	209.72	$5,197.35	$3,495.50	$13,987.57	
13	December	Fill Formatting Only	578.77	$938.35	$7,961.63	$17,134.76	
14	January	Fill Without Formatting / Fill Months	781.45	$59,416.19	$62,275.01	$229,537.71	
15							

Select the Fill Formatting method just to overwrite the series and then copy the formats from the source frame.

You can see that in Figure C, the fill handle canceled the series values. Additionally, the action reverted to the original data and applied the formats from A3 to the destination. This technique is not preferable to Format Painter, so you're not going to have to pick the goal set, which may be difficult for a wide one.

Figure C

	A	B	C	D	E	F	G
1		Smith	Jones	Michaels	Hancock	Totals	
2	January	$4,212.64	$6,795.69	$2,148.78	$4,611.14	$17,768.25	
3	February	$3,194.08	$3,449.36	$9,020.05	$7,401.84	$23,065.33	
4	March	$3,000.00	$2,332.71	$8,507.84	$4,224.17	$18,064.72	
5	April	$2,500.00	$2,804.82	$9,078.84	$7,620.23	$22,003.89	
6	May	$2,989.75	$2,504.17	$4,263.65	$2,706.73	$12,464.30	
7	June	$3,200.34	$5,426.36	$5,325.03	$4,494.94	$18,446.68	
8	July	$6,912.61	$4,229.14	$6,361.90	$5,936.46	$23,440.11	
9	August	$4,596.56	$5,936.79	$3,222.88	$3,304.52	$17,060.75	
10	September	$7,529.99	$7,673.70	$2,862.51	$3,831.45	$21,897.65	
11	October	$5,188.08	$9,840.23	$2,489.00	$6,686.40	$24,203.70	
12	November	$3,085.00	$2,209.72	$5,197.35	$3,495.50	$13,987.57	
13	December	$3,656.00	$4,578.77	$938.35	$7,961.63	$17,134.76	
14	TOTALS	$50,065.06	$57,781.45	$59,416.19	$62,275.01	$229,537.71	
15							

2: Use Paste to Copy Formatting

Another fast copy technique uses the function Paste. The Format Painter once again works well with a limited selection, but this trick is useful when copying formats to a whole column or row:

- Select the source cell and press [Ctrl]+C.

- Select anywhere in the column or row of the destination.

- To select the whole row, click [Ctrl] + [Spacebar] to select the whole column, or [Shift] + [Spacebar]. (This only works with a blank range of data.) 2010: With the selected column or row, choose Drop-down Paste Formatting (in the Clipboard group). 2007: Choose Drop-down Paste Special, and click Formats in the Paste section. 2003: Right-click the selected node, and pick Special Paste from the submenu. Click Formats in the Paste portion in the corresponding window.

- You can see what formats the Live Preview applies to. If you decide to apply, then click, OK.

You can also use Paste to format a new Chart. Select the source diagram, then press [Ctrl]+C. Select the destination chart, select Drop-down Paste Special, pick Sizes, and press OK.

3: Copy Styles Between Workbooks

When many workbooks use the same design cell designs, don't waste time recreating each form. Then, import the template as follows from one tab into another:

- Open a workbook source and a workbook destination.

- From the workbook for your destination, click on the Home tab on Cell Styles in the Styles group. Choose Styles from Format's menu in Excel 2003.

- Select Merge Styles at the gallery bottom.

- Select the open workbook containing the styles you want to copy in the resulting dialog.

- Click OK twice.

If you choose to use the same design template for all new workbooks, open the default workbook on Excel, book.xltx as the gateway. (In Excel 2003, open book.xlt.) Add a theme, then save a template file and close it. The workbooks based on book.xltx should have the models combined.

4: Create a Custom Format for Readable Data

Few-digit numbers are easy to interpret. Once you fall into that second thousand separators, numbers become less readable, especially if there are lots of them in your data. Fortunately, the number of digits can be reduced by a custom format, making them easier to read without changing scale. To explain this, we're going to add this unique format to the values at the bottom (so you can compare):

- choose B9: E13 and tap the Number group's dialog launcher or press [Ctrl]+1 to display the Format Cells dialog.

- On the Category list (on the Number tab), pick Custom.

- Enter $# #, "M," in the Type Control; string format, as shown in Figure D. Combined with the two comma characters, the pound sign displays a character in million-position, if any. The M component displays, to denote millions, a literal character M.

- Tap OK to see the results in Figure E.

Figure D

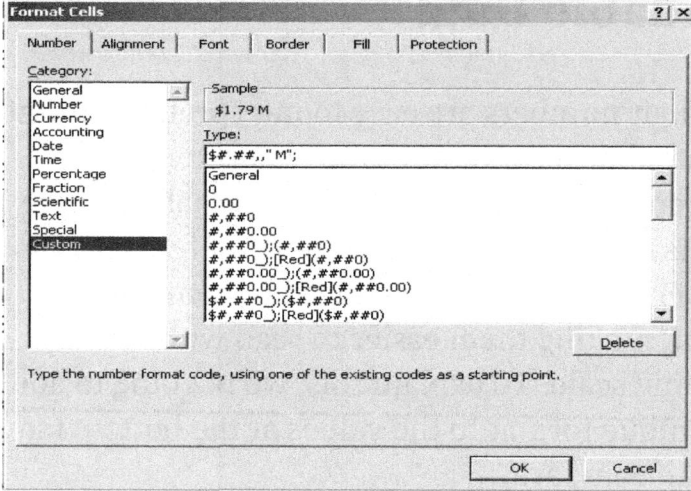

Add this custom format string.

Figure E

	A	B	C	D	E
1		Smith	Jones	Michaels	Hancock
2	North	$1,793,906	$1,941,972	$2,949,318	$1,379,624
3	South	$141,897	$3,901,525	$3,031,663	$1,791,178
4	East	$7,692,284	$763,317	$1,366,237	$182,908
5	West	$2,643,272	$1,089,000	$1,559,500	$21,253
6	Totals	$12,271,359	$7,695,814	$8,906,718	$3,374,963
7					
8		Smith	Jones	Michaels	Hancock
9	North	$1.79 M	$1.94 M	$2.95 M	$1.38 M
10	South	$.14 M	$3.9 M	$3.03 M	$1.79 M
11	East	$7.69 M	$.76 M	$1.37 M	$.18 M
12	West	$2.64 M	$1.09 M	$1.56 M	$.02 M
13	Totals	$12.27 M	$7.7 M	$8.91 M	$3.37 M
14					

5: Create a Cell Style that Indicates a Purpose

Identifying purpose using a Cell Style helps users acclimatize faster. This also offers a convenient way to maintain the integrity of the company. You could use color to distinguish input and label cells, for example. Using a Cell Model is an easy means of bringing the tradition to function. Let's demonstrate this idea by making an Input Cell Style:

- Click on the Home tab and then select Cell Types in Category Types. Choose Style from Format menu in Excel 2019, and skip to # 3.

- At the bottom of the list, tap the New cell style.

- Enter a name for the theme, such as InputCell, in the resulting dialog box.

- Tap Format. In Excel 2019, tap Modify.

- Tap the Border tab and select the Outline option in the Presets section.

- Tap the File tab and select light blue.

- Tap OK to view the chosen formats shown in Figure F.

- Tap, OK again.

Figure F

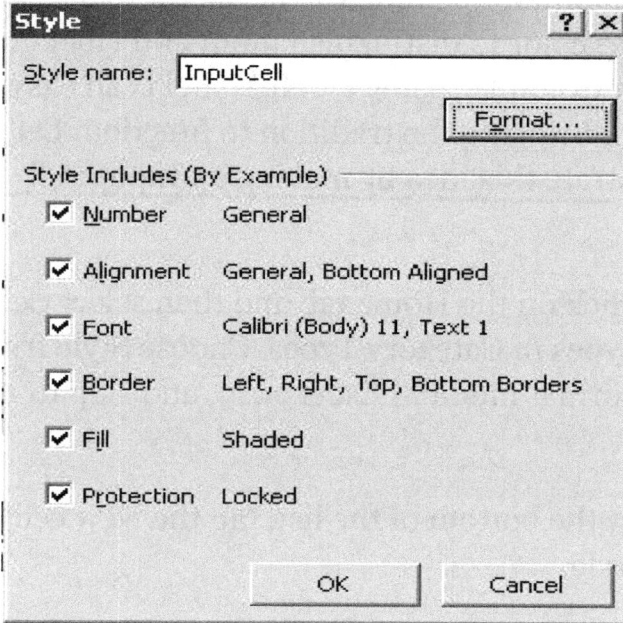

Style

Style name: InputCell

Format...

Style Includes (By Example)

☑ Number   General

☑ Alignment   General, Bottom Aligned

☑ Font   Calibri (Body) 11, Text 1

☑ Border   Left, Right, Top, Bottom Borders

☑ Fill   Shaded

☑ Protection   Locked

OK   Cancel

WAYS TO SOLVE COMMON PRINTING ISSUES IN EXCEL

Occasionally, a spreadsheet doesn't print well, maybe because you did it portrait instead of printing in landscape format. A file area might not have been printed, or maybe it required more paper than expected to print. Regardless of what went wrong, the following tips will help you avoid several printing issues in this program.

For this guide, we use Excel 365, but almost every piece of advice relates to the earlier two versions of Excel. Try doing these steps before you print the spreadsheet next time you encounter problems in the printout.

How to Verify the Orientation?

Look at the orientation before printing that document. To test the landscape, click on the Page Configuration tab to see the normal orientation you would need to look at, and pick Orientation. Then, check the margins of the page by selecting Margins next to Orientation. To that, the total amount of prints selects the option Narrow, or select the option Custom Margins and set the values you want. Leave some room for your margins whilst at it.

How to Put a Page Break in Place?

When you take a printout of it, an Excel document with several columns or rows that break at the wrong location, to solve this, the split is added. To put a horizontal break, pick the row you need to split the printout in. Choose the entire column to put one, which is vertical.

Then press on Breaks at the Web Interface, and pick Insert Web Split. Select the corresponding column or row, click on Breaks, and select Remove Page Break to get rid of it. In the event you need to get rid of many page breaks, under the Breaks section, there is an option to reset all of these.

How to Look at Preview?

You see, to get an idea of what the printout looks like. To enter the Print mode in which you will display your text, press the Ctrl and F2 keys at once. You may then move between sample sites. When you're done, simply click the left arrow at the top to go back to the normal view.

How to Set or Clear the Spreadsheet's Print Area?

Upon incorrect printing of the paper, setting or removing this region will help correct it. You'd like to remove it if you haven't set the right print area. Select Print Area under Page Layout, and select Clear Print Area to do so.

MOVE OR COPY WORKSHEETS OR WORKSHEET DATA

You may use the moving or copying sheet command to move or copy whole worksheets (also referred to as sheets) in the same or different workbooks to other locations. The Cut and Copy commands can be used to move or copy a portion of the data to other worksheets or workbooks.

Move a Worksheet within a Workbook

Choose the worksheet tab and drag it to where you want it.

Caution: Check any formulas or charts that refer to the sheet data when moving a sheet to another workbook, because moving the sheet may cause errors or produce unintended results in your data. Likewise, if you move a sheet referenced by 3-D references, the calculation could include or leave out data on the sheet.

Copy a Worksheet in the same Workbook

- Click CTRL and drag the worksheet tab to the tab location you want.

OR

- Right-click on the worksheet tab and pick Move or Copy.

- Choose the "Create a copy checkbox."

- Under the before sheet, pick where you want to place the copy.

- Choose OK.

HOW TO CREATE A DATABASE FROM AN EXCEL SPREADSHEET?

More definitely, you're used to using Microsoft Excel for activities such as writing papers, predictions, and budgets. Excel, however, is much more effective than this. It can be used to create a database that is a searchable-an Excel database.

Excel's storage features are really powerful. Indeed, Excel can be used to create a simple searchable database and be used to create a proper relational database. A relational database consists of a master table connecting to its slave tables, also known as child tables.

How Does a Relational Database Work?

Excel is structured in such a way as to be easily compatible with databases. At the very least, according to PC World, a database is essentially a list of related objects. That's sort of a spreadsheet. When associating the items in the database, they create records within multiple record groupings.

A single document may be the equivalent of a row in a spreadsheet, whereas a document set may be the equivalent of a table in a spreadsheet. The connection can be difficult to ignore.

You're arguably looking at a database when you have a spreadsheet, all alone. It is definitely not a relational database, though. You need to merge a master spreadsheet with slave spreadsheets, or plain tables, to construct a relational database.

An Example of a Database

Say, for instance, you decide to store your identification documents in your computer, and you do this or the documents of any other individual. If it's your driver's license, it's among many other people's driver's licenses at the DMV.

There will be information on your certificates, such as your name, height, weight, ethnicity, hair and eye color, date of birth, address, dates of issue and expiration, and type of certificate.

You will note that many people can share a name, gender, address, and overall description. That's why license numbers are available to make each license unique. That's what is considered a Key Field in database parlance, and is used to link a database to other databases connected with it; these are often known as relational databases.

The Master Database

The master folder should hold all the details concerning your driver's license. One or more child repositories with more knowledge regarding particular children are described using the Main Sector.

Some may have an individual's driving violations, while others may have previously-held addresses, and so on. This kind of relationship is known in database parlance as a one-to-many relationship because each driver can have many different addresses and violations. However, only one driver can connect the addresses and the violations.

Other types of relationships exist, such as one-to-one and many-to-many-for example, a customer database, and the discount rates they enjoy. Because each customer can have only one discount at a time, that is a one-to-one relationship. Suppose the database consisted of customers and the products they buy. In that case, customers could have more than one product, and more than one customer could buy the products – which would be a multiple to many relationships.

What Is a Relational Database for?

The most obvious explanation of why a database such as this could be important is to prevent repeating your data on a tablet. That can be resource-intensive – especially as regards time. The most critical reason to use a database is that it helps you scan the data using filters to locate relevant details and use it to produce reports.

How to Create a Simple Database in Excel?

Describing your data is the first step to creating a searchable spreadsheet. To describe your data, you will need labels, and these will go into the first row of your table. Let's make that your spreadsheet the very first row.

The function of headings in a proper database is pretty much the same as that of fields. -- row in the spreadsheet represents a single database record when each column has the values in a single group.

The header of the row on row one must be frozen. Click on the row header located at the right edge of the second row to do this. Go to the Display tab at the top of the Excel program on the ribbon, and look at the Freeze Panes segment on the screen. An arrow is below.

Click on that arrow and select the "Freeze Top Row" option from the pop-up drop-down menu. This will mean that the top row will always be visible while scrolling through your spreadsheet. In this way, you know within which type of data all fall.

Enter Your Data

It's time to get your data in. Do so in as many rows as you felt you need to. The arrow keys should be as easy as pressing the enter key to helping you maneuver through your spreadsheet when verifying entry into every cell.

You may have entered your data in another document where the character on the tab separates it, for example, in Microsoft Word. You can then simply copy it and paste it into your spreadsheet. Click on the cell marked A2 to paste it into your database, and press Ctrl + V on your keyboard. The details will be pasted beneath the headers.

There is a button at the top left corner of your worksheet that you can use to select all the cells in your spreadsheet. This button is found where the headings of the column and the row intersect. Click on this button, and it will pick all the cells in your worksheet. Switch to the Data tab on the ribbon. There you will find the group labeled "Sort and Filter." A funnel-like button named "Filter" button is found.

Using Filters in Columns

You should find an arrow on the right-hand side of any column heading when you position your cursor there. Click on it, and you'll get a column menu with options you can use to filter things. You may use filters for texts and numbers, or arrange them into either ascending or descending order or show only rows in the specified column that follow the filter requirements.

In front of "Pick Everything' is a checkbox. Uncheck it and then trigger the checkbox next to the values for filtering your results. It will only contain data for certain meanings.

Filter According to Conditions

If you choose to filter by circumstances, pick a function from either the "Text Filters" or "Digit Filters." You might go with items like values between two different values or greater than or less than a specified value, etc. For each condition, there are "And" and "Or" buttons, so you can compound your criteria to be mutually exclusive or additive.

Click on the "Yes" tab to filter your results. You'll only see the rows in the column you've selected that match your filter conditions.

Turn Off Filtering

If you want to switch off the filtering, press the filter button at the top right corner of the column's specified heading, which filters you want to toggle off. This way, you turn off the filtering for that column without affecting the rest of the spreadsheet. If you want to turn off all the filtering, simply select the "Clear" option, and all your data will return to their original state.

CONTROL DATA ENTRY FORMATS WITH INPUT MASKS

Do you know you can help people Access Desktop database by offering input masks for areas that contain data that is always formatted? For example, you may use an input mask to ensure that people type properly written phone numbers into a field of phone numbers.

The input mask just affects the acceptance of data by Access-the mask does not change how data is stored; controlled by the data type of the field and other properties

About Input Masks

An input mask is a character string that shows the appropriate format for the input values. The input masks can be used in table fields, query fields, and form and report controls. The input mask is stored as the property of an object.

When the input values format must be compatible, you use an input mask. For example, you may be using an input mask with a field that stores phone numbers, so Access requires ten input digits. If anyone enters a phone number without the area code, so Entry does not write the data until the data is applied to the area code.

The Three Parts of an Input Mask

One compulsory part and two optional parts are composed of input masks, and a semicolon separates each part. Each part has its purpose as follows:

- The first part is absolutely compulsory. This contains the mask characters or string (character series) along with placeholders and basic details such as brackets, lines, and hyphens.

- The second part is optional, referring to the embedded mask characters and how they are stored in the field. When the second part is set to 0, the data are stored in the characters, and the characters will only be displayed and not stored if set to 1; setting the second part to 1 might save storage space in the database.

- Also optional is the third part of the input mask, and it indicates a single character or space used as a placeholder. Access makes use of the underscore (_) by default. Insert it in the third part of your mask if you want to use another character.

For instance, this is an input mask for telephone numbers in the U.S. format: (999) 000-000;0;-:

- Two placeholder characters, 9 and 0, are used on the mask. The nine displays an optional digit (which allows accessing an area code optional), and every 0 displays a compulsory figure.

- In the second part of the mask, input 0 indicates that the mask characters are stored along with the information.

- 3rd part of the input mask mandated that a hyphen (-) rather than the underscore (_) is to be utilized as the placeholder character.

Characters that Define Input Masks

The table below lists the placeholder and actual characters for an input mask and describes how the data entry is controlled:

Character	Explanation
0	User must enter a digit (0 to 9).
9	User can enter a digit (0 to 9).
#	User can enter a digit, space, plus or minus sign. If skipped, Access enters a blank space.
L	User must enter a letter.
?	User can enter a letter.
A	User must enter a letter or a digit.
a	User can enter a letter or a digit.
&	User must enter either a character or a space.
C	User can enter characters or spaces.
. , : ; - /	Decimal and thousands placeholders, date and time separators. The character you select depends on your Microsoft Windows regional settings.
>	Coverts all characters that follow to uppercase.
<	Converts all characters that follow to lowercase.
!	Causes the input mask to fill from left to right instead of from right to left.
\	Characters immediately following will be displayed literally.
""	Characters enclosed in double quotation marks will be displayed literally.

When to Avoid Using Input Masks in Access

Input masks are not appropriate in any case, however helpful they can be. If conditions refer to you: Do not use an input mask:

- Occasionally, people need to insert details which do not suit the mask. An input mask makes no exceptions.

- Use Date Picker control with Date / Time field. The Date Picker function is not consistent with the input masks.

Add an Input Mask to a Table Field Using the Input Mask Wizard

You may use input masks with fields set to the data types Text, Number (except for ReplicationID), Currency, and Date / Time.

Note: If you use a Date / Time field input mask, the Date Picker control for that field becomes unavailable.

255

- In the Navigation Pane, right-click the table and tap Design View on the shortcut menu.

- Tap the field where you want to add the input mask.

- Under Field Properties, on the General tab, tap the Input Mask property box.

- Tap Build to launch the Input Mask Wizard button.

- Pick the type of mask you want to include in the Input Mask list.

- Tap Test it and enter data to check the view of the mask.

- Press Next to keep the input mask unchanged.

- Select an option for how to store the data.

- Tap Finish and save your changes.

Add an Input Mask to a Query

Right-click the query you want to change in the Navigation Pane and click the Design View menu on the shortcut menu.

1. Place the pointer in the column in the query design grid for the field you want to change.

2. You can place the cursor for this field in any line.

3. Press F4 to open the field property document.

4. On the General page, under Field Properties, tap the Input Mask property box.

5. To start the Input Mask Wizard, click the Build Builder button, then follow the wizard instructions.

Add an Input Mask to a Form or Report Control

1. Right-click the type or text you wish to modify in the Navigation Window, and press the Interface View button on the shortcut screen.

2. Right-click the control you want to change, then in the shortcut menu, click Properties.

3. On the All tab, tap the Input Mask property box.

4. To start the Input Mask Wizard, click the Build Builder button, then follow the wizard's instructions.

Create Custom Input Masks

While the Input Mask Wizard offers input masks for the most common formatting needs, you may want to better adapt your input masks to your needs. You may either change the default masks of the input mask wizard by modifying the default masks or manually adjust the input mask property to a region in which the mask is added.

Customize Input Masks from the Input Mask Wizard

Open the object in Design View and press the area where the custom input mask is to be inserted.

1. Tap the Build Builder button to start the Input Mask Wizard.

2. Tap Edit List.

3. The dialog box Configure Input Mask Wizard is shown.

4. In the dialog, move to a new record and enter a new description in the text box on Description.

5. Enter characters and placeholders in the Input Mask text box using the permitted characters from the table list.

6. Tap the Mask Type down arrow and choose a suitable mask type.

7. Tap Close. The new input mask is mentioned.

Customize Input Masks from the Field Property Setting

1. Right-click the item in the Navigation Window, and press the Interface View button on the shortcut screen.

2. Click the field where the custom input mask is to be produced.

3. Tap the text box Input Mask in the field Property section, then type your custom mask.

4. Press CTRL+S to save your changes.

For the Number and Currency fields, you have to type the input mask definition manually.

Examples of Input Masks

The explanations in the table below illustrate several ways you can use the input masks.

This input mask	Provides this type of value	Notes
(000) 000-0000	(206) 555-0199	In this case, you must enter an area code because that section of the mask (000, enclosed in parentheses) uses the 0 placeholder.
(999) 000-0000!	(206) 555-0199 ( ) 555-0199	In this case, the area code section uses the 9 placeholder, so area codes are optional. Also, the exclamation point (!) causes the mask to fill in from left to right.
(000) AAA-AAAA	(206) 555-TELE	Allows you to substitute the last four digits of a U.S. style phone number with letters. Note the use of the 0 placeholder in the area code section, which makes the area code mandatory.
#999	-20 2000	Any positive or negative number, no more than four characters, and with no thousands separator or decimal places.
>L????L?000L0	GREENGR339M3 MAY R 452B7	A combination of mandatory (L) and optional (?) letters and mandatory numbers (0). The greater-than sign forces users to enter all letters in uppercase. To use an input mask of this type, you must set the data type for the table field to **Text** or **Memo**.
00000-9999	98115- 98115-3007	A mandatory postal code and an optional plus-four section.
>L<?????????????	Maria Pierre	A first or last name with the first letter automatically capitalized.
ISBN 0-&&&&&&&&&-0	ISBN 1-55615-507-7	A book number with the literal text, mandatory first and last digits, and any combination of letters and characters between those digits.
>LL00000-0000	DB51392-0493	A combination of mandatory letters and characters, all uppercase. Use this type of input mask, for example, to help users enter part numbers or other forms of inventory correctly.

Using Input Masks for Email Addresses

Since email addresses differ greatly in the number of characters they include, input masks are not reliable to ensure accurate centering of email addresses.

Instead, we recommend using the properties of the Validation rule and Text Validation.

The validation rule shown in the table below ensures that you enter the email address with one or more characters, then a "@" sign, then one or more characters, then a period, then one or more characters.

Alex@example.com, for example, would be permitted, but alex@example, com or alex@example would not.

If you enter a validation rule-free email address, Access will not accept the input and display the Validation Text property message.

If no text is inserted in the property box Validation Code, Access will show a default document.

Property	Setting
Validation Rule	Is Null Or ((Like "*?@?*.?*") And (Not Like "*[,;]*"))
Validation Text (optional)	Please enter the email address with an '@' sign and the full domain name (for example, 'frank@contoso.com').

CONCLUSION

Microsoft Excel is an application known as the spreadsheet. You can handle numerical data through a spreadsheet. Calculations can be performed as well as analysis and forecast. So what does Microsoft Excel let you do? Essentially it will enable you to conduct a variety of similar tasks in the spreadsheet.

You're presented with a grid-like page when you load up Excel; this is a termed worksheet. All your details will be stored here, and numerous worksheets form a workbook. The grid consists of a series of rows and columns, and data is entered in single cells. For example, you can multiply the value in one cell by the value in a different cell. You can apply all sorts of mathematical functions to the cells.

Microsoft Excel is used for several tasks; you can build a table for anything basic, like keeping track of your monthly outputs. Through doing this, you can hold a running list on exactly how much you pay per month.

Alternatively, you may be working in a business environment and be using Excel more seriously. In this case, your spreadsheet applications can become complex and require a great deal of understanding here. Engineering is another good example where Excel is very functional to make work easier. Math functions can be applied to your data. This might be something simple like summing up a data column or something more complex, like the quantitative analysis.

Also, Excel allows you to create a database as you wish. You'd best choose anything devoted to database management or Microsoft Access; since Excel is part of the MS Office suite of programs, it can connect with other software inside the package. For example, you might want to transfer your Excel data to MS Access, or vice versa.

Excel is an extremely powerful tool that is useful to home and business alike.

ONE LAST THING TO DO

First, I will like to say a big thank you to you for taking the time to buy and read this book. I took a lot of time to craft a guide like this to help you. It means a lot to me that you can read this book. I hope I'm able to solve many of your excel difficulty for you.

We need your help

If you have found some of the information in this book useful, you will undoubtedly benefit greatly from it in the future. With Excel, you can optimize your work and personal time, and you will probably feel grateful when you get great satisfaction in specific work situations.

So if you feel inspired and want to help others with "Excel 2020", here are some beautiful actions you can do immediately:

1. Write a short 5-star review on Amazon
2. Teach someone the commands you learned on Excel through your "Excel 2020". In this way, you will have the advantage to metabolize your knowledge better, and you

will also receive the gratitude of the person you helped

3. Recommend this book to anyone who wants to learn Excel
4. You give a copy of "Excel 2020" to a family member, a friend, in the office, a colleague who wants to learn more about Excel.

I read all the reviews personally so I can get your feedback and make this book even better.

Thanks again for your support!

Made in the USA
Middletown, DE
03 February 2021